D1145795

On
Literature

'J Hillis Miller's slim but ambitious volume is both a timely intervention in debates about the contemporary value of literature (precisely because attentive to the time of reading) and an engaging addition to a body of work dedicated to the maintenance of an essential mustery, a "secular magic", at the heart of the western literary tradition.'

Brian Dillon, *Times Literary Supplement*

Praise for the series

"... allows a space for distinguished thinkers to write about their passions."
The Philosophers' Magazine

"... deserves high praise."
Boyd Tonkin, *The Independent* (UK)

"This is clearly an important series. I look forward to reading future volumes."
Frank Kermode, author of *Shakespeare's Language*

"... both rigorous and accessible."
Humanist News

"... the series looks superb."
Quentin Skinner

"... an excellent and beautiful series."
Ben Rogers, author of *A.J. Ayer: A Life*

"Routledge's *Thinking in Action* series is the theory junkie's answer to the eminently pocketable Penguin 60s series."
Mute Magazine (UK)

"Routledge's new series, *Thinking in Action*, brings philosophers to our aid ..."
Evening Standard (UK)

"... a welcome new series by Routledge."
Bulletin of Science, Technology and Society

J. HILLIS MILLER

M
45.
M4

On *Pop*
Literature

Routledge
Taylor & Francis Group

LONDON AND NEW YORK

First published 2002
by Routledge
11 New Fetter Lane, London EC4P 4EE

Simultaneously published in the USA and Canada
by Routledge
29 West 35th Street, New York, NY 10001

Routledge is an imprint of the Taylor & Francis Group

© 2002 J. Hillis Miller

Typeset in Joanna by RefineCatch Ltd, Bungay, Suffolk
Printed and bound in Great Britain by
Biddles Ltd, Guildford and King's Lynn

British Library Cataloguing in Publication Data
A catalogue record for this book is available from the British Library

Library of Congress Cataloguing in Publication Data
Miller, J. Hillis (Joseph Hillis), 1928-
     On literature / J. Hillis Miller.
         p. cm. - (Thinking in action)
     Includes bibliographical references and index.
     1. Literature.   2. Books and reading.   I. Title   II. Series.
     PN45.M495 2002
     801'3 - dc21   2002021331

ISBN 0-415-26124-4 (hbk)
ISBN 0-415-26125-2 (pbk)

Another for
Dorothy

And all the rest is literature.

Paul Verlaine

Acknowledgements

I am grateful for help with this book from many people, especially Julian Wolfreys, Jason Wohlstadter, and Barbara Caldwell, my "Senior Editor" and invaluable assistant at the University of California, Irvine. I thank Simon Critchley for first suggesting that I might write this book for the series he edits, as well as for his careful reading of the manuscript. I am grateful also to the co-editor of the series, Richard Kearney, for a helpful reading of the manuscript. Muna Khogali and Tony Bruce, of Routledge, have been unfailingly generous and courteous. Tony Bruce read the manuscript with care and made useful suggestions.

A preliminary version of some of the ideas in this book, especially those in Chapter 4, was presented as a lecture for the Koehn Endowed Lectureship at the University of California, Irvine, in Febuary 2001. The lecture was called "On the Authority of Literature." Subsequently, the talk was given as the first annual Lecture on Modern Literature for the Department of English at Baylor University in April, 2001. The lecture was then printed there as a pamphlet for local circulation. I am grateful to my host and sponsor at Baylor, Professor William Davis, for his many kindnesses. Different versions of the talk were given at two conferences, in August 2001, in the People's Republic of China: at a triennial conference of the Chinese Association for Sino-Foreign Literary and

Cultural Theory, held in Shenyang, and at an International Symposium on Globalizing Comparative Literature, sponsored by Yale and Tsinghua Universities. I thank Professor Wang Ning for arranging these invitations and for many other courtesies. A German translation will be published as my contribution to a research project on "representative validity," sponsored by the Zentrum für Literaturforschung in Berlin. I especially thank Ingo Berensmeyer, as well as other colleagues in Berlin, for the chance to try out my ideas on them. A Bulgarian translation will be published in a Festschrift for Simeon Hadjikosev, of Sofia University. I thank Ognyan Kovachev for inviting me, and for other kindnesses. Altogether, my preliminary ideas for Chapter 4 and for some other germs of this book have had the benefit of many helpful comments and reactions.

Finally, I thank the dedicatee of this book for suffering once more through my ordeals of composition. She had to endure my faraway look, my dreamy absentmindedness. I was dwelling again in imagination on the other side of Alice's looking-glass or on the deserted island where the Swiss Family Robinson made such an enchanting home. It has taken me a good many months to figure out what to say about that experience.

Sedgwick, Maine
December 15, 2001

One

FAREWELL LITERATURE?

The end of literature is at hand. Literature's time is almost up. It is about time. It is about, that is, the different epochs of different media. Literature, in spite of its approaching end, is nevertheless perennial and universal. It will survive all historical and technological changes. Literature is a feature of any human culture at any time and place. These two contradictory premises must govern all serious reflection "on literature" these days.

What brings about this paradoxical situation? Literature has a history. I mean "literature" in the sense we in the West use the word in our various languages: "literature" (French or English) "letteratura" (Italian), "literatura" (Spanish), "Literatur" (German). As Jacques Derrida observes in *Demeure: Fiction and Testimony*, the word literature comes from a Latin stem. It cannot be detached from its Roman-Christian-European roots. Literature in our modern sense, however, appeared in the European West and began in the late seventeenth century, at the earliest. Even then the word did not have its modern meaning. According to the Oxford English Dictionary, the word "literature" was first used in our current sense only quite recently. Even a definition of "litera-ture" as including memoirs, history, collections of letters, learned treatises, etc., as well as poems, printed plays, and novels, comes after the time of Samuel Johnson's dictionary (1755). The restricted sense of literature as just poems, plays, and novels is even more recent. The word "literature" is defined by Johnson exclusively in the now obsolescent sense of "Acqaintance with 'letters' or books; polite or humane learning; literary culture." One example the OED gives is as late as 1880: "He was a man of very small literature." Only by the third definition in the OED does one get to:

Joseph & Thomes Wharton

Literary production as a whole; the body of writings produced in a particular country or period, or in the world in general. Now also in a more restricted sense, applied to writing which has claim to consideration on the grounds of beauty of form or emotional effect.

This definition, says the OED, "is of very recent emergence both in England and France." Its establishment may be conveniently dated in the mid-eighteenth century and associated, in England at least, with the work of Joseph and Thomas Wharton (1722–1800; 1728–90). They were hailed by Edmund Gosse, in an essay of 1915–16 ("Two Pioneers of Romanticism: Joseph and Thomas Wharton"), as giving literature its modern definition. Literature in that sense is now coming to an end, as new media gradually replace the printed book.

WHAT HAS MADE LITERATURE POSSIBLE?

What are the cultural features that are necessary concomitants of literature as we have known it in the West? Western literature belongs to the age of the printed book and of other print forms like newspapers, magazines, and periodicals generally. Literature is associated with the gradual rise of almost universal literacy in the West. No widespread literacy, no literature. Literacy, furthermore, is associated with the gradual appearance from the seventeenth century onward of Western-style democracies. This means regimes with expanded suffrage, government by legislatures, regulated judicial systems, and fundamental human rights or civil liberties. Such democracies slowly developed more or less universal education. They also allowed citizens more or less free access to printed materials and to the means of printing new ones.

This freedom, of course, has never been complete. Various forms of censorship, in even the freest democracies today, limit the power of the printing press. Nevertheless, no technology has ever been more effective than the printing press in breaking down class hierarchies of power. The printing press made democratic revolutions like the French Revolution or the American Revolution possible. The Internet is performing a similar function today. The printing and circulation of clandestine newspapers, manifestoes, and emancipatory literary works was essential to those earlier revolutions, just as email, the Internet, the cell phone, and the "hand-held" will be essential to whatever revolutions we may have from now on. Both these communication regimes are also, of course, powerful instruments of repression.

The rise of modern democracies has meant the appearance of the modern nation-state, with its encouragement of a sense of ethnic and linguistic uniformity in each state's citizens. Modern literature is vernacular literature. It began to appear as the use of Latin as a *lingua franca* gradually disappeared. Along with the nation-state has gone the notion of national literature, that is, literature written in the language and idiom of a particular country. This concept remains strongly codified in school and university study of literature. It is institutionalized in separate departments of French, German, English, Slavic, Italian, and Spanish. Tremendous resistance exists today to the reconfiguration of those departments that will be necessary if they are not simply to disappear.

The modern Western concept of literature became firmly established at the same time as the appearance of the modern research university. The latter is commonly identified with the founding of the University of Berlin around 1810, under the guidance of a plan devised by Wilhelm von Humboldt. The modern research university has a double charge. One is *Wissenschaft*, finding out the truth about everything. The other is *Bildung*, training citizens (originally almost exclusively male ones) of a given nation-state in the ethos appropriate for that state. It is perhaps an exaggeration to say that the modern concept of literature was created by the research university and by lower-school training in preparation for the university. After all, newspapers, journals, non-university critics and reviewers also contributed, for example Samuel Johnson or Samuel Taylor Coleridge in England. Nevertheless, our sense of literature was strongly shaped by university-trained writers. Examples are the Schlegel brothers in Germany, along with the whole circle of critics and philosophers within German Romanticism. English examples would include William Wordsworth, a Cambridge graduate. His "Preface to Lyrical Ballads" defined poetry and its uses for generations. In the Victorian period Matthew Arnold, trained at Oxford, was a founding force behind English and United States institutionalized study of literature. Arnold's thinking is still not without force in conservative circles today.

Arnold, with some help from the Germans, presided over the transfer from philosophy to literature of the responsibility for *Bildung*. Literature would shape citizens by giving them knowledge of what Arnold called "the best that is known and thought in the world." This "best" was, for Arnold, enshrined in canonical Western works from Homer and the Bible to Goethe or Wordsworth. Most people still first hear that there is such a thing as literature from their school teachers.

Universities, moreover, have been traditionally charged with the storage, cataloguing, preservation, commentary, and interpretation of literature through the accumulations of books, periodicals, and manuscripts in research libraries and special collections. That was literature's share in the university's responsibility for *Wissenschaft*, as opposed to *Bildung*. This double responsibility was still very much alive in the literature departments of The Johns Hopkins University when I taught there in the 1950s and 1960s. It has by no means disappeared today.

Perhaps the most important feature making literature possible in modern democracies has been freedom of speech. This is the freedom to say, write, or publish more or less anything. Free speech allows everyone to criticize everything, to question everything. It confers the right even to criticize the right to free speech. Literature, in the Western sense, as Jacques Derrida has forcefully argued, depends, moreover, not just on the right to say anything but also on the right not to be held responsible for what one says. How can this be? Since literature belongs to the realm of the imaginary, whatever is said in a literary work can always be claimed to be experimental, hypothetical, cut off from referential or performative claims. Dostoevsky is not an ax murderer, nor is he advocating ax murder in *Crime and Punishment*. He is writing a fictive work in which he imagines what it might be like to be an ax murderer. A ritual formula is printed at the beginning of many modern detective stories: "Any resemblance to real persons, living or dead, is purely coincidental." This (often false) claim is not only a safeguard against lawsuits. It also codifies the freedom from referential responsibility that is an essential feature of literature in the modern sense.

A final feature of modern Western literature seemingly contradicts the freedom to say anything. Even though democratic freedom of speech in principle allows anyone to say anything, that freedom has always been severely curtailed, in various ways. Authors during the epoch of printed literature have *de facto* been held responsible not only for the opinions expressed in literary works but also for such political or social effects as those works have had or have been believed to have had. Sir Walter Scott's novels and Harriet Beecher Stowe's *Uncle Tom's Cabin* have in different ways been held responsible for causing the American Civil War, the former by instilling absurdly outmoded ideas of chivalry in Southern gentry, the latter by decisively encouraging support for the abolition of slavery. Nor are these claims nonsensical. *Uncle Tom's Cabin* in Chinese translation was one of Mao Tse Tung's favorite books. Even today, an author would be unlikely to get away before a court of law with a claim that it is not he or she speaking in a given work but an imaginary character uttering imaginary opinions.

Just as important as the development of print culture or the rise of modern democracies in the development of modern Western literature, has been the invention, conventionally associated with Descartes and Locke, of our modern sense of the self. From the Cartesian *cogito*, followed by the invention of identity, consciousness, and self in Chapter 27, Book II, of Locke's *An Essay Concerning Human Understanding*, to the sovereign I or *Ich* of Fichte, to absolute consciousness in Hegel, to the I as the agent of the will to power in Nietzsche, to the ego as one element of the self in Freud, to Husserl's phenomenological ego, to the *Dasein* of Heidegger, explicitly opposed to the Cartesian ego, but nevertheless a modified form of subjectivity, to the I as the agent of performative utterances such as "I promise" or "I bet" in the speech act theory of J. L. Austin and others, to the subject not as something abolished but as a problem to be interrogated within deconstructive or postmodern thinking – the whole period of literature's heyday has depended on one or another idea of the self as a self-conscious and responsible agent. The modern self can be held liable for what it says, thinks, or does, including what it does in the way of writing works of literature.

Literature in our conventional sense has also depended on a new sense of the author and of authorship. This was legalized in modern copyright laws. All the salient forms and techniques of literature have, moreover, exploited the new sense of selfhood. Early first-person novels like *Robinson Crusoe* adopted the direct presentation of interiority characteristic of seventeenth-century Protestant confessional works. Eighteenth-century novels in letters exploited epistolary presentations of subjectivity. Romantic poetry affirmed a lyric "I." Nineteenth-century novels developed sophisticated forms of third-person narration. These allowed a double simultaneous presentation by way of indirect discourse of two subjectivities, that of the narrator, that of the character. Twentieth-century novels present directly in words the "stream of consciousness" of fictional protagonists. Molly Bloom's soliloquy at the end of *Ulysses* is the paradigmatic case of the latter.

THE END OF THE PRINT AGE

Most of these features making modern literature possible are now undergoing rapid transformation or putting in question. People are now not so certain of the unity and perdurance of the self, nor so certain that the work can be explained by the authority of the author. Foucault's "What is an Author?" and Roland Barthes's "The Death of the Author" signaled the end of the old tie between the literary work and its author considered as a unitary self, the real person William Shakespeare or Virginia Woolf. Literature itself has contributed to the fragmentation of the self.

Forces of economic, political, and technological globalization are in many ways bringing about a weakening of the nation-state's separateness, unity, and integrity. Most countries are now multilingual and multi-ethnic. Nations today are seen to be divided within as well as existing within more permeable borders. American literature now includes works written in Spanish, Chinese, Native American languages, Yiddish, French, and so on, as well as works written in English from within those groups, for example African-American literature. Over sixty minority languages and cultures are recognized in the People's Republic of China. South Africa after apartheid has eleven official languages, nine African languages along with English and Afrikaans. This recognition of internal division is ending literary study's institutionalization according to national literatures, each with its presumedly self-enclosed literary history, each written in a single national language. The terrible events of the mid-twentieth century, World War II and the Holocaust, transformed our civilization and Western literature with it. Maurice Blanchot and others have even argued persuasively that literature in the old sense is impossible after the Holocaust.

In addition, technological changes and the concomitant development of new media are bringing about the gradual death of literature in the modern sense of the word. We all know what those new media are: radio, cinema, television, video, and the Internet, soon universal wireless video.

A recent workshop I attended in the People's Republic of China (PRC) brought together American literary scholars and representatives of the Chinese Writers Association. At that meeting it became evident that the most respected and influential Chinese writers today are those whose novels or stories are turned into one or another television series. The major monthly journal printing poetry in the PRC has in the last decade declined in circulation from an amazing 700,000 to a "mere" 30,000, though the proliferation of a dozen or more new influential poetry journals mitigates that decline somewhat and is a healthy sign of diversification. Nevertheless, the shift to the new media is decisive.

Printed literature used to be a primary way in which citizens of a given nation state were inculcated with the ideals, ideologies, ways of behavior and judgment that made them good citizens. Now that role is being increasingly played, all over the world, for better or for worse, by radio, cinema, television, VCRs, DVDs, and the Internet. This is one explanation for the difficulties literature departments have these days in getting funding. Society no longer needs the university as the primary place where the national ethos is inculcated in citizens. That work used to be done by the humanities departments in colleges and universities, primarily through literary study. Now it is increasingly done by television, radio talk shows, and by cinema. People cannot be reading Charles Dickens or Henry James or Toni Morrison and at the same time watching television or a film on VCR, though some people may claim they can do that. The evidence suggests that people spend more and more time watching television or surfing the Internet. More people, by far, probably, have seen the recent films of novels by Austen, Dickens, Trollope, or James than have actually read those works. In some cases (though I wonder how often), people read the book because they have seen the television adaptation. The printed book will retain cultural force for a good while yet, but its reign is clearly ending. The new media are more or less rapidly replacing it. This is not the end of the world, only the dawn of a new one dominated by new media.

One of the strongest symptoms of the imminent death of literature is the way younger faculty members, in departments of literature all over the world, are turning in droves from literary study to theory, cultural studies, postcolonial studies, media studies (film, television, etc.), popular culture studies, Women's studies, African-American studies, and so on. They often write and teach in ways that are closer to the social sciences than to the humanities as traditionally conceived. Their writing and teaching often marginalizes or ignores literature. This is so even though many of them were trained in old-fashioned literary history and the close reading of canonical texts.

These young people are not stupid, nor are they ignorant barbarians. They are not bent on destroying literature nor on destroying literary study. They know better than their elders often do, however, which way the wind is blowing. They have a deep and laudable interest in film or popular culture, partly because it has done so much to form them as what they are. They also have a proleptic sense that traditional literary study is on the way to being declared obsolete by society and by university authorities. This will probably happen not in so many words. University administrators do not work that way. It will happen by the more effective device of withdrawing funding in the name of "necessary economies" or "downsizing." Departments of classics and modern languages other than English, in United States universities, will go first. Indeed, they are in many universities already going, initially through amalgamation. Any United States English department, however, will soon join the rest, if it is foolish enough to go on teaching primarily canonical British literature under the illusion that it is exempt from cuts because it teaches texts in the dominant language of the country.

Even the traditional function of the university as the place where libraries store literature from all ages and in all languages, along with secondary material, is now being rapidly usurped by digitized databases. Many of the latter are available to anyone with a computer, a modem, and access to the Internet through a server. More and more literary works are freely available online, through various websites. An example is "The Voice of the Shuttle," maintained by Alan Liu and his colleagues at the University of California at Santa Barbara (http://vos.ucsb.edu/). The Johns Hopkins "Project Muse" makes a large number of journals available (http://muse.jhu.edu/journals/index_text.html).

A spectacular example of this making obsolete the research library is the William Blake Archive website (http://www.blakearchive.org/). This is being developed by Morris Eaves, Robert Essick, and Joseph Viscomi. Anyone anywhere who has a computer with an Internet connection (I for example on the remote island off the coast of Maine where I live most of the year and am writing this) may access, download, and print out spectacularly accurate reproductions of major versions of Blake's *The Marriage of Heaven and Hell* and some of his other prophetic books. The original versions of these "illuminated books" are dispersed in many different research libraries in England and the United States. Formerly they were available only to specialists in Blake, to scholars with a lot of money for research travel. Research libraries will still need to take good care of the originals of all those books and manuscripts. They will less and less function, however, as the primary means of access to those materials.

Literature on the computer screen is subtly changed by the new medium. It becomes something other to itself. Literature is changed by the ease of new forms of searching and manipulation, and by each work's juxtaposition with the innumerable swarm of other images on the Web. These are all on the same plane of immediacy and distance. They are instantaneously brought close and yet made alien, strange, seemingly far away. All sites on the Web, including literary works, dwell together as inhabitants of that non-spatial space we call cyberspace. Manipulating a computer is a radically different bodily activity from holding a book in one's hands and turning the pages one by one. I have earnestly tried to read literary works on the screen, for example Henry James's *The Sacred Fount*. I happened at one moment not to have at hand a printed version of that work, but found one on the Web. I found it difficult to read it in that form. This no doubt identifies me as someone whose bodily habits have been permanently wired by the age of the printed book.

WHAT THEN IS LITERATURE?

If, on the one hand, literature's time (as I began by saying) is nearly up, if the handwriting is on the wall, or rather if the pixels are on the computer screen, on the other hand, literature or "the literary" is (as I also began by saying) universal and perennial. It is a certain use of words or other signs that exists in some form or other in any human culture at any time. Literature in the first sense, as a Western cultural institution, is a special, historically conditioned form of literature in the second sense. In the second sense, literature is a universal aptitude for words or other signs to be taken as literature. About the political and social utility, import, effectiveness of literature I shall write later, in Chapter 4, "Why Read Literature?" At this point my goal is to identify what sort of thing literature is.

What then is literature? What is that "certain use of words or other signs" we call literary? What does it mean to take a text "as literature"? These questions have often been asked. They almost seem like non-questions. Everyone knows what literature is. It is all those novels, poems, and plays that are designated as literature by libraries, by the media, by commercial and university presses, and by teachers and scholars in schools and universities. To say that does not help much, however. It suggests that literature is whatever is designated as literature. There is some truth to that. Literature is whatever bookstores put in the shelves marked "Literature" or some subset of that: "Classics," "Poetry," "Fiction," "Mysteries," and so on.

It is nevertheless also the case that certain formal features allow anyone dwelling within Western culture to say with conviction, "This is a novel," or "This is a poem," or "This is a play." Title pages, aspects of print format, for example the printing of poetry in lines with capitals at the beginning of each line, are as important in segregating literature from other print forms as internal features of language that tell the adept reader he or she has a literary work in hand. The co-presence of all these features allows certain collocations of printed words to be taken as literature. Such writings can be used as literature, by those who are adept at doing that. What does it mean to "use a text as literature"?

Readers of Proust will remember the account at the beginning of *À la recherche du temps perdu* (*Remembrance of Things Past*) of the magic lantern his hero, Marcel, had as a child. It projected on Marcel's walls and even on his doorknob images of the villainous Golo and the unfortunate Geneviève de Brabant, brought into his bedroom from the Merovingian past. My version of that was a box of stereopticon photographs, probably by Matthew Brady, of American Civil War scenes. As a child, I was allowed to look at these at my maternal grandparents' farm in Virginia. My great-grandfather was a soldier in the Confederate Army. I did not know that then, though I was told that a great-uncle had been killed in the Second Battle of Bull Run. I remember in those awful pictures as much the dead horses as the bodies of dead soldiers. Far more important for me as magic lanterns, however, were the books my mother read to me and that I then learned to read for myself.

When I was a child I did not want to know that *The Swiss Family Robinson* had an author. To me it seemed a collection of words fallen from the sky and into my hands. Those words allowed me magical access to a pre-existing world of people and their adventures. The words transported me there. The book wielded what Simon During, in *Modern Enchantments*, calls in his subtitle, "the cultural power of secular magic." I am not sure, however, that secular and sacred magics can be all that easily distinguished. This other world I reached through reading *The Swiss Family Robinson*, it seemed to me, did not depend for its existence on the words of the book, even though those words were my only window on that virtual reality. The window, I would now say, no doubt shaped that reality through various rhetorical devices. The window was not entirely colorless and transparent. I was, however, blissfully unaware of that. I saw through the words to what seemed to me beyond them and not dependent on them, even though I could get there in no other way than by reading those words. I resented being told that the name on the title page was that of the "author" who had made it all up.

Whether many other people have had the same experience, I do not know, but I confess to being curious to find out. It is not too much to say that this whole book has been written to account for this experience. Was it no more than childish naiveté, or was I responding, in however childish a way, to something essential about literature? Now I am older and wiser. I know that The Swiss Family Robinson was written in German by a Swiss author, Johann David Wyss (1743–1818), and that I was reading an English translation. Nevertheless, I believe my childhood experience had validity. It can serve as a clue to answering the question, "What is literature?"

LITERATURE AS A CERTAIN USE OF WORDS

Literature exploits a certain potentiality in human beings as sign-using animals. A sign, for example a word, functions in the absence of the thing named to designate that thing, to "refer to it," as linguists say. Reference is an inalienable aspect of words. When we say that a word functions in the absence of the thing to name the thing, the natural assumption is that the thing named exists. It is really there, somewhere or other, perhaps not all that far away. We need words or other signs to substitute for things while those things are temporarily absent.

If I am out walking, for example, and see a sign with the

word "Gate," I assume that somewhere nearby is an actual gate that I can see with my eyes and grasp with my hands to open or shut it, once I get in sight of it and get my hands on it. This is especially the case if the word "Gate" on the sign is accompanied by a pointing arrow and the words "¼ mile," or something of the sort. The real, tangible, usable gate is a quarter of a mile away, out of sight in the woods. The sign, however, promises that if I follow the arrow I shall soon be face to face with the gate. The word "gate" is charged with signifying power by its reference to real gates. Of course, the word's meaning is also generated by that word's place in a complex differential system of words in a given language. That system distinguishes "gate" from all other words. The word "gate," however, once it is charged with significance by its reference to real gates, retains its significance or signifying function even if the gate is not there at all. The sign has meaning even if it is a lie put up by someone to lead me astray on my walk. The word "Gate" on the sign then refers to a phantom gate that is not there anywhere in the phenomenal world.

Literature exploits this extraordinary power of words to go on signifying in the total absence of any phenomenal referent. In Jean-Paul Sartre's quaint terminology, literature makes use of a "non-transcendent" orientation of words. Sartre meant by this that the words of a literary work do not transcend themselves toward the phenomenal things to which they refer. The whole power of literature is there in the simplest word or sentence used in this fictitious way.

Franz Kafka testified to this power. He said that the entire potentiality of literature to create a world out of words is there in a sentence like, "He opened the window." Kafka's first great masterpiece, "The Judgment," uses that power at the end of its first paragraph. There the protagonist, Georg Bendemann, is shown sitting "with one elbow propped on his desk . . . looking out the window at the river, the bridge, and the hills on the farther bank with their tender green."

Stéphane Mallarmé gave witness to the same amazing magic of words, in this case a single word. In a famous formulation, he pronounced: "I say: a flower! and, outside the forgetting to which my voice relegates any contour, in the form of something other than known callices, musically there rises, the suave idea itself, the absence of all bouquets."

Words used as signifiers without referents generate with amazing ease people with subjectivities, things, places, actions, all the paraphernalia of poems, plays, and novels with which adept readers are familiar. What is most extraordinary about literature's power is the ease with which this generation of a virtual reality occurs. The little story of my imaginary walk in the woods to encounter a misleading, perhaps a sinisterly prevaricating, sign is a small example of that.

It might be objected that many literary works, perhaps modernist or postmodernist ones especially, though by no means uniquely, deliberately resist translation into an internal imaginary spectacle. Mallarmé's poems, Joyce's *Finnegans Wake*, the strange works of Raymond Roussel, or the late poems of Wallace Stevens are examples. Such works force the reader to pay attention to the linguistic surface, rather than going through it to some virtual reality to which it gives access. Even in such works, however, the reader struggles to imagine some scene or other. Mallarmé's poem about his wife's fan, "Éventail (de Madame Mallarmé)," is a poem about that fan, just as his "Tombeau (de Verlaine)" is about Verlaine's tomb and the weather around it on a certain day. Stevens's "Chocorua to Its Neighbor" is pretty rarefied, all right, but it is still readable as an imaginary conversation between a star and a real mountain. That is Mt. Chocorua, in New Hampshire, near which the American philosopher, William James, used to spend his summers. Early drafts of *Finnegans Wake* help readers to orient themselves, for example, in one particularly opaque passage by knowing that beneath various layers of outrageous puns and portmanteau words it is recounting the Tristan and Isolde story, with Tristan in modern guise as "a handsome six foot rugby player." Part of the pleasure of Roussel's *Impressions d'Afrique* is the struggle, by no means wholly unsuccessful, to disentangle the various bewilderingly intertwined narrative strands. The virtual realities such works invent or discover are pretty weird, but so, in their own ways, are even the most traditionally "realistic" fictions. Examples, to be discussed later, are Anthony Trollope's novels, with their strange assumption that each character has intuitive understanding of what other characters are thinking. Moreover, even the most opaque or idiosyncratic literary construction tends to generate the fictive illusion of a speaking voice.

A literary work is not, as many people may assume, an imitation in words of some pre-existing reality but, on the contrary, it is the creation or discovery of a new, supplementary world, a metaworld, a hyper-reality. This new world is an irreplaceable addition to the already existing one. A book is a pocket or portable dreamweaver. I refer in this figure to two series of books popular some decades ago, "Pocket Books" and "Portable" books – *The Portable Conrad*, *The Portable Dorothy Parker*, *The Portable Hemingway*, and so on. These names signal the portability of modern books as generators of alternative worlds. You can carry these little devices wherever you go. They will still go on working their magic when you read them, anywhere, anytime. These modern small books are quite different from Renaissance folios, for example the Shakespeare Folio. Those big books were meant to stay in one place, most often in a rich person's private library.

Literature makes exorbitant and large-scale use of the propensity words possess to go on having meaning even in the absence of any ascertainable, phenomenally verifiable, referent. A beguiling circumstantiality tends to characterize literature. An example is the specification that it was "a Saturday afternoon in November" at the opening of *The Return of the Native*. Another is the spurious hiding of what are implied to be real street names, with only the first and last letters given, as if something needs to be hidden, in the first sentence of *Crime and Punishment*. No way exists from the opening sentence of Henry James's *The Wings of the Dove* to tell whether or not Kate Croy was a real person: "She waited, Kate Croy, for her father to come in . . ."

Often the illusion that the text is a chronicle of real people and events, not a fictive concoction, is reinforced by the use of real place names. An unwary reader, however, is likely to be fooled by a bogus circumstantiality. Kate Croy's father's house exists in a real place, the Chelsea region of London, but a search of London maps fails to turn up a Chirk Street, where the narrator says that house was located. It sounds as if there ought to be a Chirk Street in Chelsea but there is not. Goswell Road, however, is a real street in the Finsbury section of East London, but no Mr Pickwick ever opened a window and looked out upon it, in a passage to which I shall return. To alter Marianne Moore's aphorism defining poetry as imaginary gardens with real toads in them, *Pickwick Papers* names a real garden with an imaginary toad. The name "Chirk Street" is like a plausible-enough-looking entry in a fictitious telephone book, that just does not happen to correspond to any real telephone. Literature derails or suspends or redirects the normal referentiality of language. Language in literature is derouted so that it refers only to an imaginary world.

The referentiality of the words a work uses, however, is never lost. It is inalienable. The reader can share in the work's world by way of this referentiality. Trollope's novels carry over into the imaginary place they create (or discover) all sorts of verifiable information about Victorian middle-class society and about human life, for example about courtship and marriage, as we all in one way or another know it. *The Swiss Family Robinson* is full of accurate information about animals, birds, fish, and plants. Those historical and "realistic" details, however, are, in both cases, transposed, transfigured. They are used as a means to transport the reader, magically, from the familiar, the verisimilar, to another, singular place that even the longest voyage in the "real world" will not reach. Reading is an incarnated as well as a spiritual act. The reader sits in his or her chair and turns material pages with bodily hands. Though literature refers to the real world, however, and though reading is a material act, literature uses such physical embedment to create or reveal alternative realities. These then enter back into the ordinary "real" world by way of readers whose beliefs and behavior are changed by reading – sometimes for the better, perhaps sometimes not. We see the world through the literature we read, or, rather, those who still have what Simon During calls "literary subjectivity" do that. We then act in the real world on the basis of that seeing. Such action is a performative rather than a constative or referential effect of language. Literature is a use of words that makes things happen by way of its readers.

I have used, and will go on using, the word "magic" to name the power that words on the page have to open up a virtual reality when they are read as literature. Simon During, in *Modern Enchantments: The Cultural Power of Secular Magic*, already referred to, has admirably traced the history of magic shows and entertainments, from the Renaissance to the early twentieth century. As part of this history he has discussed the relation of magic to literature. He is interested primarily in works like Hoffmann's *Kater Murr* or Raymond Roussel's *Impressions d'Afrique*. Such works have a more or less direct relation to magic shows. Among these he mentions the Alice books, important points of reference later on in this present book. The basic fiction of Alice passing through the looking-glass echoes magic stage practices and traditions. Moreover, the scenes of the vanishing Cheshire cat and the baby made to sneeze with pepper may be covert references, as During has suggested, to a famous nineteenth-century magic stage show, done with mirrors, called "Pepper's Ghost." John Fisher, in *The Magic of Lewis Carroll*, has detailed Carroll's knowledge of nineteenth-century staged illusions.

During does not explicitly observe, however, that all literary works, whether or not they overtly refer to magic practices, can be usefully thought of as a species of magic. A work of literature is an abracadabra or hocus pocus that opens a new world. During has something to say about the way cinema extended magic shows, for example by being based in part on magic lanterns that were long a part of magic stage presentations. Eventually cinema put staged magic out of business. It had the stronger force. During also does not observe, however, that modern communications technologies, from trick photography, to the telephone, to cinema, to radio, to television, to recordings on disks, tapes, or CDs, to the computer connected to the Internet, fulfill in reality old dreams of magic communication, at a temporal or spatial distance, with the living or with the dead. I can, any time I like, hear Glenn Gould play Bach's *Goldberg Variations* with fingers long since turned to dust. I can even hear Alfred Lord Tennyson reciting his poems. Talk about raising ghosts!

As Laurence Rickels has shown, in the early days of both the telephone and the tape recorder, people believed they were hearing the voices of the dead (usually their mother's) behind the voices of the living, or through the static, on a telephone connection or a tape recording. These tele-technologies have gradually displaced not only magic stage assemblages, but also that other fading form of secular magic: literature. Cinema, television, CDs, VCRs, MP3 gadgets, computers, and the Internet have become our dominant far-seeing and far-hearing conjurers, sorcerers, prestidigitators, animators of talking heads. These devices are, in short, our chief purveyors of magic shows. They have incalculable power to determine ideological belief.

One place where the way any literary work is a form of conjuring emerges explicitly is in the first words of George Eliot's *Adam Bede* (1859):

> With a single drop of ink for a mirror, the Egyptian sorcerer undertakes to reveal to any chance comer far-reaching visions of the past. This is what I undertake to do for you, reader. With this drop of ink at the end of my pen, I will show you the roomy workshop of Mr Jonathan Burge, carpenter and builder in the village of Hayslope, as it appeared on the eighteenth of June in the year of our Lord 1799.

As Neil Hertz has observed, George Eliot and her readers

would have known in 1859 that the Egyptian sorcerer in question was Abd-El-Kadir El-Maghrabee, who lived in Cairo earlier in the century. He is mentioned, Hertz reminds us, in a brief work by J. L. Borges, written in the 1930s, "The Mirror of Ink." What is striking about Eliot's figure is the way it uses the figure of a magic trick to name the power not of a Hoffmannian fantasy nor of a work of twentieth-century "magic realism," but of a paradigmatic example of good old-fashioned mimetic realism, complete with circumstantial dates and places. The analogy also brilliantly transposes the magic practice of Abd-El-Kadir (who used a small pool of ink in the palm of his hand as a visionary mirror) into the ink at the end of the writer's pen that forms the words on the page we are at that moment reading. These words are a mirror in what might be called a Carrollian sense, that is, not as a reflection of something here and now, but as a magic looking-glass that the reader penetrates to enter a new reality on the other side, distant in time and space: the workshop of Mr Jonathan Burge in Hayslope on June 18, 1799. The sentences are both constative and performative. They name Jonathan Burge's roomy workshop constatively. They promise to "show" it to the reader, "as it appeared." In making the promise, the words fulfill the promise. The "roomy workshop" arises "magically" before the reader's mind's eye, more and more circumstantially so as he or she reads the elaborate description of it that follows these opening words.

Two

"OPEN SESAME"

For me the opening sentences of literary works have special force. They are "Open Sesames" unlocking the door to that particular work's fictive realm. All it takes is a few words, and I become a believer, a seer. I become the fascinated witness of a new virtual reality. More accurately, I become a disembodied observer within that reality. "There was a Boy; ye knew him well, ye cliffs/And islands of Winander!" does it for me with Wordsworth's "The Boy of Winander." "Mrs Dalloway said she would buy the flowers herself," does it for me with Virginia Woolf's *Mrs Dalloway*. "He was an inch, perhaps two, under six feet, powerfully built, and he advanced straight at you with a slight stoop of the shoulders, head forward, and a fixed from-under stare which made you think of a charging bull," does it for me with Conrad's *Lord Jim*. "I caught this morning morning's minion, king-/dom of daylight's dauphin, dapple-dawn-drawn Falcon," does it for me with Gerard Manley Hopkins's "The Windhover." "I struck the board and cried, 'No more,'" does it for me with George Herbert's "The Collar."

Sophocles's *Oedipus the King* opens ominously with a question from Oedipus to the procession of Theban priests and citizens: "My sons! Newest generation of this ancient city of Thebes! Why are you here?" Oedipus's first words raise the questions of generation, of fatherhood and sonship. Such themes are fundamental in Oedipus's story of patricide and incest. Oedipus's habit of asking questions, and of not being satisfied until he finds answers, gets him into a lot of trouble, to put it mildly. In that same opening speech, he says: "Here I am, myself, world-famous Oedipus." He presumably refers to his fame for solving the Sphynx's riddle. Oedipus becomes truly world-famous, but not quite for the reasons he thinks. The whole play is contained in miniature in Oedipus's first speech.

In each case I have cited, the opening words instantly transport me into a new world. All the words that come after in each work do no more than give me further information about a realm I have already entered. The words are radically inaugural. They are the creation, in each case, of a new, alternative universe. These words are a miniature, secular, all-too-human version of God's "Let there be light" in Genesis.

A long litany of such beginnings could be cited. I cite a few more out of admiration for their generative power and to illustrate the way each one is a miniature genesis. I put them down pell-mell, in deliberate randomness, as they come to mind. This disorder stresses their heterogeneity. They are stored, so to speak, in separate partitions within that strange organic hard-drive, my memory. I shall have something to say about each, either now or later:

> At the beginning of July, during an extremely hot spell, towards evening, a young man left the closet he rented from tenants in S-----y Lane, walked out to the street, and slowly, as if indecisively, headed for the K-----n Bridge.
> (Fyodor Dostoevsky, *Crime and Punishment*)

Someone must have slandered Josef K., for one morning, without having done anything truly wrong, he was arrested.

(Franz Kafka, *The Trial*)

Of Man's First Disobedience, and the Fruit
Of the Forbidden Tree, whose mortal tast
Brought Death into the World, and all our woe . . .

(John Milton, *Paradise Lost*)

Peach tree soft and tender,
how your blossoms glow!
The bride is going to her home,
she well befits this house.

(Chinese *Classic of Poetry*, VI,
"Peach Tree Soft and Tender")

Sitting beside the road, watching the wagon mount the hill toward her, Lena thinks, "I have come from Alabama: a fur piece. All the way from Alabama a-walking. A fur piece."

(William Faulkner, *Light in August*)

A sudden blow: the great wings beating still
Above the staggering girl, her thighs caressed
By the dark webs . . .

(W. B. Yeats, "Leda and the Swan")

I am a sick man . . . I am a spiteful man. I am an unattractive man. I believe my liver is diseased.

(Dostoevsky, *Notes from Underground*)

A number of features characterize these inaugural moments. They tend to be abrupt or irruptive. Each is a sudden intrusion on the reader, wherever he or she happens to be when the book is opened. They command attention. Having read these opening words, the reader wants to go on reading. The words whisk the reader into a new place. He or she is enchanted in an instant and wants to explore this brave new world further. This can only be done by reading further, and so the reader is "hooked."

These opening moments tend, moreover, in one way or another to be violent. This is so not only in the way they suddenly interrupt whatever the reader was thinking or doing until the moment the book was opened. They also tend to be violent beginnings to tales of violence. This may be the relatively justified and benign violence of God's relation to the self in the poems by Herbert or Hopkins, or the violence of sexuality in *Light and August* and "Leda and the Swan," or the violent stories of transgression told in works like *Lord Jim*, or the psychological violence of the really weird character who speaks in *Notes from Underground*. I first read *Notes from Underground* when I was a sophomore in college. I remember saying to myself, in my sophomoric way, "Here at last is someone like myself, someone who speaks to me of my secret sense of myself." *anticipative*

The irruptive, transgressive violence of these beginnings is often proleptic or synecdochic, part for whole, of the work that follows. The climactic violence of *Lord Jim*, for example, when the hero allows himself to be shot, as expiation at last for his unwilling complicity in asocial acts, seems somehow foreshadowed in that image of Jim as like a charging bull. The violence of literature tends to involve either sexuality, or death, or both.

About violence in *The Swiss Family Robinson* I shall say something later. I add here and now, however, as a point of special importance, that this violence is experienced as pleasurable. This is true however ashamed we may be of the pleasure in vicarious violence a literary work enacts for us. Literature gives pleasurable violence even though the violence may be no more than the laughter engendered by the outrageous wordplay of a work like *Alice's Adventures in Wonderland*. In the latter, for example, a chapter entitled "The Rabbit Sends in a Little Bill" turns out not to have anything to do with bills in the economic sense. The bill in question is a lizard named Bill. The Rabbit sends Bill down the chimney and Alice kicks him back up the chimney. In the Tenniel illustration, he comes flying out like a projectile. In another episode, Alice and the animals are dried off after their swim in Alice's tears by hearing the Mouse read aloud an exceedingly dry historical account. Such puns produce, in me at least, an explosion of laughter. Laughter too is violent, as Yeats and Freud knew. All literary works have something of the laughter-producing weirdness of dreams. Laughter repeats the transgression from which it would protect us, while at the same time holding the transgressive at a distance.

WHY IS LITERATURE VIOLENT?

Why all this violence in literature? Why is that violence pleasurable? It seems as though literature not only satisfies a desire for entry into virtual realities but that those virtual realities tend to enact, however covertly, an approach toward the hyperbolic violences of death, sexuality, and the subversion hidden in the irrationalities of language. At the same time, literature in one way or another protects us from those violences.

Friedrich Nietzsche, as Paul Gordon has shown in *Tragedy After Nietzsche*, held that tragedy is essentially superabundant rapture (Rausch) and that all art is essentially tragic. "If there is to be art," wrote Nietzsche in *Twilight of the Idols*, "if there is to be any aesthetic doing and observing, one *physiological pre-condition* is indispensable: rapture." "Rapture": the word means being drawn forcibly out of oneself into another realm. That other realm is by no means peaceful. It is associated in one way or another with those excessive things I have named: death, sexuality, and the irrational side of language. Literature seizes me and carries me to a place where pleasure and pain join. When I say I am "enchanted" by the virtual realities to which literary works transport me, that is a milder way of saying I am enraptured by reading those works. Literary works are in one way or another wild. That is what gives them their power to enrapture.

OPENINGS AS THE RAISING OF GHOSTS

Shakespeare's plays might almost be taken as a counterproof of what I have been saying. They typically open not with a speech by one of the main characters but by dialogue among subsidiary folk. A Shakespeare play often begins with minor characters who establish the social milieu within which the main drama will be enacted. *Hamlet*, for example, starts not with the appearance of the ghost but with a conversation between two sentinels, Bernardo and Francisco (unlikely names for Danes), on the battlements of Elsinore Castle. *Othello* begins not with Othello himself, but with a speech by Roderigo, a "gulled gentleman," victim of Iago's villainy. Shakespeare's beginnings, nevertheless, obey my law of an irruptive start in the middle of things. They instantly establish a new social space, the space within which Hamlet or Othello will work out his tragic destiny.

The opening of Hardy's *The Return of the Native* sets a scene, Egdon Heath. The heath is, the chapter title says, "A Face on which Time makes but Little Impression": "A Saturday afternoon in November was approaching the time of twilight, and the vast tract of unenclosed wild known as Egdon Heath embrowned itself moment by moment."

The openings of Mrs Dalloway, Lord Jim, Crime and Punishment, Herbert's "The Collar," Faulkner's Light in August and many other works, however, establish in a single sentence a character, often a chief protagonist. For me the character springs to life with this sentence. The personage remains alive ever afterward somewhere in my imagination, as a kind of ghost that may not be exorcized, neither alive nor dead. Such ghosts are neither material nor immaterial. They are embodied in the words on the pages in all those books on the shelves waiting to be invoked again when the book is taken down and read.

Sometimes it is not quite the first sentence that brings the character alive. The opening sentence of the second chapter of Pickwick Papers brings Mr Pickwick to life for me, along with the distinctive ironic parodic voice of Dickens himself, the "Immortal Boz," as he liked to be called. What is parodied in this case is the circumstantiality of place and date that is expected of "realist" fiction. The sentence opening the second chapter picks up the fiat lux echo in the first sentence of the novel. Here is part of that first first sentence: "The first ray of light which illumines the gloom, and converts into a dazzling brilliancy that obscurity in which the earlier history of the immortal Pickwick would appear to be involved . . ." This opening parodies not only Genesis but also the pomposities found in official biographies of "great men." It also indicates Dickens's own inaugural power as author, light-bringer. The echo of that in the beginning of the second chapter applies the same figure to Pickwick's appearance on a fine morning:

That punctual servant of all work, the sun, had just risen, and begun to strike a light on the morning of the thirteenth of May, one thousand eight hundred and twenty-seven, when Mr Samuel Pickwick burst like another sun from his slumbers, threw open his chamber window, and looked out upon the world beneath. Goswell Street was at his feet, Goswell Street was on his right hand – as far as the eye could reach, Goswell Street extended on his left; and the opposite side of Goswell Street was over the way. *postponed*

George Eliot's Dorothea Brooke, in *Middlemarch*, to give another example of a deferred beginning, does not come fully alive for me in the opening sentences. The novel opens like this: "Miss Brooke had that kind of beauty which seems to be thrown into relief by poor dress. Her hand and wrist were so finely formed that she could wear sleeves not less bare of style than those in which the Blessed Virgin appeared to Italian painters . . ." This is circumstantial enough, but what really brings Dorothea to life for me is a moment in the opening scene with her sister Celia when, against her principles, Dorothea admires the jewelry they have inherited from their mother: " 'How very beautiful these gems are!' said Dorothea, under a new current of feeling, as sudden as the gleam [that the sun has just reflected from the jewels]."

The attentive reader will note how often these openings, though I have chosen them more or less at random from those that stick in my mind, involve in one way or another either the sun or the opening of a window. Sometimes, as in *Pickwick Papers*, both motifs are present. *Mrs Dalloway*, to give a final example, a few sentences beyond the opening sentence I have cited, shows Clarissa remembering an experience of her childhood:

> What a lark! What a plunge! For so it had always seemed to her, when, with a little squeak of the hinges, which she could hear now, she had burst open the French windows and plunged at Bourton into the open air.

The beginning of the world, even these imaginary literary ones, seems naturally figured by a rising sun or by a window opening from the inside to the outside.

Such openings, in third-person narrations, are also spoken by another voice, the narrator's. Even first-person narrations are double. The "I" as narrator speaks of a past "I" whose experiences are narrated in the past tense: "I struck the board . . ." Such opening sentences create the illusion of a speaker out of nothing but words. An example is the ironic understatement of Kafka's narrative voice. That voice tells about the most grotesque or horrific events in a flat matter-of-fact tone. The opening of *Paradise Lost* establishes the poet's voice as it invokes the Muse, just as the first sentence of *Pride and Prejudice* fabricates out of a few words an ironic narrator quite different from Kafka's ironic narrator. Austen's story-teller reports, with cool objectivity, the ideological assumptions of the novel's community. It does not wholly distance itself from those assumptions: "It is a truth universally acknowledged, that a single man in possession of a good fortune must be in want of a wife."

In spite of the immense variety of these opening sentences, they all function as the instantaneous creation of a fictive world. In all these cases, the opening sentences are radically initiatory. They are a genesis, a new birth, a fresh beginning. One of the main pleasures of reading literary works is the power they give to put aside our real cares and enter another place.

What are the main features of these virtual realities that we call literary works?

First feature: they are incommensurate with one another. Each is singular, *sui generis*, strange, idiosyncratic, heterogeneous. Literary works are "counter, original, spare, strange," to borrow a formulation from Gerard Manley Hopkins. That strangeness estranges them from one another. One might even think of them as so many Leibnizian windowless monads, or as Leibnizian "incompossible" worlds, that is, as worlds that cannot logically co-exist in the same space. Each is the fictive actualization of one alternative possibility not realized in the "real world." Each is an irreplaceably valuable supplement to the real world.

Stressing literature's strangeness is a point of some importance, since much literary study (not to speak of much journalistic reviewing) has always had as one of its main functions covering that strangeness over, as the Swiss family Robinson killed or domesticated the animals, birds, and fish on their island. Literary study hides the peculiarity of literary language by accounting for it, naturalizing it, neutralizing it, turning it into the familiar. This usually means seeing in it as in one way or another a representation of the real world. Whether this accounting takes the form of relating the work to its author, or of trying to demonstrate that it is typical of its historical time and place, or characteristic of the class, gender, and race of its author, or of seeing it as a mirroring of the material and social world, or of relating it to conceptual generalizations about the way literary language works, the unspoken goal is to appease the conscious or unconscious fear people have of literature's true strangeness. We fear the way each work is incomparable.

Literature as Virtual Reality

To affirm that each work has its own truth, a truth different from the truth of any other work, sets what I am saying not only against mimetic or referential definitions of literature, but also against Heideggerian notions of literature or of "poetry" as what he calls the "setting-forth-of-truth-in-the-work." For Heidegger the truth set forth in the work is universal. It is the truth of Being. That truth is not something unique to the work, with a singular truth for each work. My definition of literature is closer to Derrida's explicitly anti-Heideggerian "concept" (it is not exactly a concept) of a poem. In "Che cos'è la poesia?," which may be crudely translated as "What Thing is Poetry?" and in the subsequent interview, "Istrice 2: Ick bünn all hier" (both reprinted in translation in *Points . . .: Interviews, 1974–1994*), a poem is figured as a hedgehog rolled up in a ball. (The strange German is Derrida's citation of Heidegger's citation of a sentence in the Grimm fairy tale of "The Hare and the Hedgehog." In this story the hedgehog beats the hare in a race by sending the female hedgehog ahead to be waiting at the finish line. It is an example, Derrida says, of the "always already there.") The hedgehog image is a catachresis, as Derrida says, for what is idiomatic about each literary work. One form this takes is the approach toward coincidence of its meaning and the materiality of its letters. Derrida's refusal to translate the idiomatic Italian title of the first essay and his insistence on the "str" sound in the admirable Italian word for hedgehog, "istrice," in the interview, is an example of one form of specificity: dependence on the idiom of a particular language. For me too, each work is a separate space, protected on all sides by something like quills. Each work is closed in on itself, separated even from its author. The work is also separated from the "real world" and from any unified supernal world which all works might be presumed to put to work.

No doubt I am here, by making a conceptual analysis, committing again the error against which I warn. It cannot be denied that literary theory contributes to that death of literature the first sentence of this book announces. Literary theory arose in its contemporary form just at the time literature's social role was weakening. It was an oblique response to that weakening. If literature's power and role could be taken for granted as still in full force, it would not be necessary to theorize about it. The greatest ancient treatise on what we today would call literature, Aristotle's *Poetics*, appeared at the time Greek tragedy, not to speak of the epic (Aristotle's chief examples of "poetry"), were in their decline. In a similar way, the remarkable twentieth-century theoretical reflections on the nature of literature appeared just at the time literature in the modern sense of the word was in the process of fading as a primary force in Western culture. I am thinking of all those theorists from Sartre, Benjamin, Lukács, and Blanchot down to de Man, Derrida, Jameson, Butler, and the rest, not to speak of those statements by creative writers like Mallarmé and Proust who anticipated later twentieth-century reflections by theorists on the essence of the literary.

The efflorescence of literary theory signals the death of literature. That Routledge editors should have invited me to write a book "on literature" is a symptom of this. They would not have thought of making such a request if literature were not widely perceived these days as problematic. Many people see literature as perhaps in mortal jeopardy, certainly as something that can no longer simply be taken for granted. Theory both registers the imminent death of literature, which of course cannot die, and at the same time helps make that death-without-death happen.

This takes place by an implacable law that says you can see clearly something that is deeply embedded in your culture only when it is in the act of receding into the historical distance. Maurice Blanchot already quietly recognized that vanishing and its primary cause in an essay of 1959, "The Song of the Sirens: Encountering the Imaginary." Speaking of the novel as the primary modern literary form, Blanchot wrote:

> It is no small thing to make a game of human time and out of that game to create a free occupation, one stripped of all immediate interest and usefulness, essentially superficial and yet in its surface movement capable of absorbing all being. But clearly, if the novel fails to play this role today, it is because technics has transformed men's time and their ways of amusing themselves.

I shall return in Chapter 3 to this question of "technics." I shall turn also to Blanchot's notion of the way the *récit*, as opposed to the novel, is oriented not toward amusement but toward what he calls "the imaginary" or "literary space (l'espace littéraire)." The latter phrase is the title of a book by Blanchot.

A person can enter "l'espace littéraire," the space, for example, of *Crime and Punishment* or of *Pride and Prejudice*, in no other way than by reading the work. All the reading in the world of Russian or English history or of the biographies of Dostoevsky or Austen, or of literary theory, valuable as such knowledge is, will not prepare you for what is most essential, that is, most idiosyncratic, about these works. Henry James expressed eloquently the uniqueness of each author's work in a famous passage in the preface to *The Portrait of a Lady*:

The house of fiction has in short not one window, but a million – a number of possible windows not to be reckoned, rather; every one of which has been pierced, or is still pierceable, in its vast front, by the need of the individual vision and by the pressure of the individual will. These apertures, of dissimilar shape and size, hang so, all together, over the human scene that we might have expected of them a greater sameness of report than we find. They are but windows at their best, mere holes in a dead wall, disconnected, perched aloft; they are not hinged doors opening straight upon life. But they have this mark of their own that at each of them stands a figure with a pair of eyes, or at least with a field-glass, which forms, again and again, for observation, a unique instrument, insuring to the person making use of it an impression distinct from every other.

LITERATURE IS PERFORMATIVE UTTERANCE

Second feature: since a literary work refers to an imaginary reality, it follows that it makes a performative rather than a constative use of words. "Performative" and "constative" are terms from speech act theory. On the one hand, a constative statement names some state of affairs, as in the assertion, "It is raining outside." Such a sentence can, in principle at least, be verified as true or false. A performative utterance, on the other hand, is a way of doing things with words. It does not name a state of affairs, but brings about the thing it names. For example, in the right circumstances a couple is married when a minister or some other duly appointed person says, "I pronounce you man and wife." Sentences in literary works, such as the inaugural statements I have cited, for example, "She waited, Kate Croy, for her father to come in . . . ," look like constative statements describing a possibly true state of affairs. However, since the state of affairs does not exist or at any rate is not reachable except through the words, those words are actually performative. They bring Kate Croy, waiting in exasperation for her father, into existence for the reader. Every sentence in a literary work is part of a chain of performative utterances opening out more and more of an imaginary realm initiated in the first sentence. The words make that realm available to the reader. Those words at once invent and at the same time discover (in the sense of "reveal") that world, in a constantly repeated and extended verbal gesture.

The imaginary realm opened by a literary work is not simply "made available" to the reader, however. The performative dimension of the work's words demands a response from the reader. Right reading is an active engagement. It requires a tacit decision to commit all one's powers to bringing the work into existence as an imaginary space within oneself. The reader must utter, in response to the work's invocation, another performative speech act: "I promise to believe in you." The famous opening sentence of Herman Melville's *Moby Dick* makes that double performative, demand invoking a response, explicit. This is also another of those sentences that brings an imaginary character to life: "Call me Ishmael." Though this sentence might be read as a permissive: "You may call me Ishmael, if you like," or as an evasion, "My name is not really Ishmael, but that is the pseudonym I ask you to call me by," its strongest reading would see it as a peremptory demand: "I command you to call me Ishmael." The reader can only assent or dissent from this demand. He or she must say, "I agree to call you Ishmael" or "I won't do it. That sounds silly." Tacitly uttering the first responsive performative is the formal acceptance of a contract. This saying "Yes" is the "Open Sesame!" that gives the reader access to all the rest of Melville's huge work. If you agree to call the narrator Ishmael, you can enter the work. Otherwise not. Some such response to a demand that the reader accept the particular rules of a given work is necessary to all acts of reading.

LITERATURE KEEPS ITS SECRETS

Yet another feature of literary works follows from the condition that we can gain access to the unique world each reveals only by reading the words on the page. We can only know of that world what the words tell us. No other place exists where we might go to get further information. A novel, a poem, or a play is a kind of testimony. It bears witness. Whatever the narrative voice says is accompanied by an implicit (and sometimes even explicit) assertion: "I swear this is what I saw; this truly happened." The difference between literary testimony and "real" testimony is that no way exists to verify or supplement what a fictive narrator says. What a real witness in the witness box asserts can be, in principle at least, checked against the testimony of other witnesses or by other means of verification. Such checking, however, does not disqualify the witness's claim that this is what he or she saw. The witness may be speaking truly of what he or she thought was there to be seen, even if it was not. Gaps and omissions in real world testimony can nevertheless often be filled in. Literature, on the contrary, keeps its secrets.

The reader can, for example, never know just what the two parties said when Gilbert Osmond proposed to Isabel Archer and was accepted, in Henry James's *The Portrait of a Lady*. This is because James's narrator does not directly recount that event. Nor does he tell the reader what happened to Isabel when she rejoined her husband in Rome, beyond the end of the novel.

Nor can the reader ever know what was the content of Milly Theale's deathbed letter to Merton Densher, in James's *The Wings of the Dove*. This is because Kate Croy burns the letter, and the narrator does not reveal the letter's contents. The reader never knows just what were the contents of the Aspern papers, in James's novella of that name, because Miss Tina burns them before the first-person narrator can get a chance to read them. In a similar way, Baudelaire, in an example Jacques Derrida discusses, does not tell the reader whether one protagonist in the prose poem "La fausse monnaie (The Counterfeit Coin)" did or did not give the beggar a counterfeit coin.

It is, I claim, an essential feature of literature to hide secrets that may not ever be revealed. Sir Thomas Browne's example of this is the impossibility of ever knowing what song the Sirens would have sung to Ulysses, in *The Odyssey*. This is because Homer only cites the song of irresistible promise, which is not the actual song that Ulysses would have heard if he had yielded to the Sirens' enticement. Nor are these secrets, for example the ones I have mentioned, trivial or unimportant. The whole meaning of the works in question turns on what is forever hidden from the reader's knowledge. The reader would like to know, needs to know, in order fully to understand the work. An unappeased curiosity is one of the emotions generated by reading literary works, but literature keeps its secrets. We would like to know just what the Sirens' song sounded like. Hearing the Sirens' song for oneself would be the only way to know whether Ulysses was exaggerating. Knowing that, however, might be fatal, as Maurice Blanchot asserts in "The Sirens' Song." In that essay the Sirens' song is taken as an allegory of the "imaginary" and of what is dangerous about literature in general. If you were to hear the

Sirens' song you might be lured permanently away from the everyday world of mundane responsibilities. A long history can be adduced of statements in literary works themselves that express a fear of literature's seductive power. I shall refer to some later.

metaphor

LITERATURE USES FIGURATIVE LANGUAGE

One sign that literary works use language in a performative rather than purely constative way is the dependence of their creative power on figures of speech. Such figures assert a similarity between one thing and another. This similarity is often generated by words, rather than being a feature of things in themselves. Examples of the many varieties of this abound in the examples I have cited of opening sentences. Lord Jim is put before the reader in that simile asserting he is like a charging bull. In the poem from the Chinese *Classic of Poetry*, all the fragile beauty of the bride going to her new home is expressed in her juxtaposition with peach blossoms. Chinese poetry often puts a physical image and a human one side by side without asserting their relation, in a metonymical juxtaposition. The latent personification of Egdon Heath in the phrase "was embrowning itself," not to speak of the overt prosopopoeia in the word "face" in the chapter title, prepares for the extravagant personification of the heath in the rest of *The Return of the Native*'s first paragraph. Raskolnikov, in *Crime and Punishment*, is defined, in another form of metonymy, by that tiny attic room he lives in as well as by the hot weather the narrator begins by mentioning. Kate Croy's narcissism is figured when she looks at herself in the mirror. Samuel Pickwick's comic sovereignty is defined by the way he rises like the sun, while the sun is demoted to being his servant, "striking a light" for him at dawn. Lena

associa tee

Grove's inextinguishable vitality is figured in the way she is always in motion. She has already come a "fur piece" from Alabama when the reader first meets her, bearing her illegitimate child within her. The Boy of Winander is defined by the way the cliffs and islands of Winander, in another personification, "knew" him. That poem begins with an extravagant apostrophe. An apostrophe is a trope in which the speaker turns toward someone or something and hails it. In the case of apostrophes to inanimate nature, the invocation is also a personification. To say "ye knew him well, ye cliffs/ And islands of Winander!" is to animate the cliffs and islands, to imply that they might answer back, as the owls answer the boy's "mimic hootings" in the rest of the poem.

What can one say of figurative language's ubiquity in these inaugural sentences? First, they indicate, as I have said, that these new births are performed by language. No metaphors, similies, metonymies, apostrophes, or personifications exist in nature, only in collocations of words. To say that Lord Jim exists as someone who comes toward you with his head down, like a charging bull, suggests that he exists only in language. Lord Jim is not to be found anywhere in the phenomenal world, however circumstantial is Conrad's description of the pseudo-world he dwells within.

Second, these figures illustrate the extraordinary power tropes have to bring an imaginary personage to life economically and elegantly. An example is the touching juxtaposition of peach blossoms and the new bride in the poem from the Chinese. The new bride, Lord Jim, and all the horde of such literary phantoms are effects of language. To say that Jim comes toward you with his head down, like a charging bull, combines, in a way characteristic of such literary language, several different tropes in one. The locution is an invocation calling Jim's ghost to come, as Ulysses invokes the shades of dead warriors in the *Odyssey*. Saying Jim was like a charging bull is a covert apostrophe or prosopopoeia hailing or interpellating Jim as one of the absent, the imaginary or the dead, thereby personifying him. It is a catachresis transferring a name ("charging bull") to what has no proper names, that is, Jim's imagined interiority as a person.

In the case of *Lord Jim*, as in so many other literary works, the protagonist is dead when the narrator tells his or her story. Even if the protagonists are not dead at the end of the story, each already belongs to an absolute past by the time his or her book is published. Their ghostly apparitions haunt our brains and feelings, as the memory of Lord Jim haunts Marlow, the narrator of his story in *Lord Jim*, just as Marlow haunted Conrad, returning in several novels, and just as Marlow haunts the imaginations of Conrad's readers, you or me.

Third: it is true that figures of speech are an ever-present aspect of language used in its ordinary referential way, for example in newspaper headlines that often nowadays are allowed sly plays on words. Here are some real examples, the first from the *China Daily*, the rest from one issue of *USA Today*: "Medical Insurance undergoes Surgery"; "'Green power' gets second wind" (a headline about windmill power); "U.S. taps Social Security reserves"; "Maturing boomers smack into the 'silver ceiling'." Nevertheless, the presence of tropes of one sort or another in almost all my opening sentences is a clue to the adept reader that he or she may be about to read something that would be defined in our culture as "literature." The puns in headlines are an understood convention. This does not make them, in most people's eyes, "poetry," though it would be possible to dispute that.

pun - play-ward

DOES LITERATURE INVENT OR DISCOVER?

Final feature of literary language: though nothing could be more important to know than whether the alternative world opened up by a given literary work is created by the words of the work or just revealed by them, nevertheless such knowledge is impossible to obtain. It is impossible to obtain because the words would look exactly the same in either case. Literature has often been defined in recent decades by its self-reflexivity or self-referentiality. Literature is said to be distinctive because it refers to itself and to its own way of working. The great linguist Roman Jakobson, for example, distinguished literary language from other uses of language by saying it manifests "the set of language toward itself." I think this feature of literature has been greatly exaggerated. By appeal to a latently sexist distinction, it has misled many readers into dismissing literature for its sterile, feminine, and boring self-reflexivity. Literature is thought to be like Kate Croy looking at herself in the mirror, as opposed to the virile use of language to refer to real things in the real world. Calling literature "self-reflexive" is a way of calling it powerless.

Most literary works, on the contrary, confess only infrequently to being something an author has made up and is manipulating. That explains why I as a child could take *The Swiss Family Robinson* as referring to a real place somewhere. Most literary works go right on talking as if the virtual realities they describe, with all their contents and events, have independent existence and are only being described, not invented. Who is to say that this is not the case, that all those alternative worlds have not been waiting somewhere for some author to find fit words for them? If so, they would go on existing there, waiting, even if their recording author were never to appear.

I think of all those novels Fyodor Dostoevsky is said to have had in his mind, no doubt wonderful works. He just never got around to writing them down. One cannot quite say that those unwritten novels did not exist. Their mode of existence, however, is exceedingly peculiar. The words of those works that *do* get written down would be exactly the same whether or not their referents pre-exist the words or not. Literature may therefore be defined as a strange use of words to refer to things, people, and events about which it is impossible ever to know whether or not they have somewhere a latent existence. That latency would be a wordless reality, knowable only by the author, waiting to be turned into words.

Three

LITERATURE AS SECULAR DREAM VISION

The definition of literature I give at the end of the previous chapter has, no doubt, little general currency these days. It was, however, widely current in a different form in the medieval tradition of the dream vision. The dream vision gets its greatest expression in Dante's (1265–1321) *Divine Comedy* (1300 ff.). It goes on having vitality as a genre as late as Percy Bysshe Shelley's (1792–1822) *The Triumph of Life* (written in 1822) and even in more recent books. Carroll's Alice books (1865, 1872) are also, after all, dream visions too. (Lewis Carroll was the pen-name of Charles Dodgson (1832–98).) A dream vision presupposes the independent existence of what the dreamer sees. Dante's speaks as though the experiences of his pilgrim had really taken place. They are only being reported in poetic language by the poet. Medieval dream visions differ from my theory of literature in that they presuppose a single supernal realm that is glimpsed in the visions, whereas for me each work gives access to a different realm.

Though dream visions are, it must be admitted, out of fashion, nevertheless several curious passages in certain great modernist authors and theorists quite surprisingly affirm one version or another of the concept of literature I have proposed. I shall cite and discuss five of these. This will indicate their variety as well as their compelling claims to be more than simply fanciful. They are more compelling, for us today, perhaps, because they belong to our modern demystified, enlightened era. They were not written in older "superstitious" times. I might have cited many more divergent versions, for example Leibniz on "incompossible worlds," or Borges on the library of Babel, or Sartre on the imaginary, or Gilles Deleuze's readings of Leibniz and Borges.

DOSTOEVSKY'S "COMPLETELY NEW WORLD"

In a short work written in 1861, Petersburg Visions in Verse and Prose, Fyodor Dostoevsky (1821–81) reports an experience he had one evening when walking home along the River Neva, in St. Petersburg. It is the experience of an alternative world:

> It seemed, in the end, that all this world, with all its inhabitants, both the strong and the weak, with all their habitations, whether beggars' shelters or gilded palaces, at this hour of twilight resembled a fantastic, enchanted vision, a dream which in its turn would instantly vanish and waste away as vapor into the dark blue heaven. Suddenly a certain strange thought began to stir inside me. I started and my heart was as if flooded in that instant by a hot jet of blood which had suddenly boiled up from the influx of a mighty sensation which until now had been unknown to me. In that moment, as it were, I understood something which up to that time had only stirred in me, but had not as yet been fully comprehended. I saw clearly, as it were, into something new, a completely new world, unfamiliar to me and known only through some obscure hearsay, through a certain mysterious

sign. I think that in those precious minutes, my real existence began . . .

This powerful passage is echoed later in a similar vision Raskolnikov has in *Crime and Punishment*. Dostoevsky goes on in the *Petersburg Visions* passage to specify that this new world is a grotesque transformation of the real one. It is the same and yet different. Dostoevsky does not speak of it as imaginary, but as real. It is more real than the putative "real world." He is the witness of this new world, not its creator or inventor. His vision also includes the sense of a laughing malicious demiurge or demon. This demon is a kind of Silenus who is pulling the strings that make these fantastic puppets dance:

> I began to look about intently and suddenly I noticed some strange people. They were all strange, extraordinary figures, completely prosaic, not Don Carloses or Posas to be sure, rather down-to-earth titular councilors and yet at the same time, as it were, sort of fantastic titular councilors. Someone was grimacing in front of me, having hidden behind all this fantastic crowd, and he was fidgeting some thread, some springs through, and these little dolls moved, and he laughed and laughed away.
>
> (xi)

All Dostoevsky's fiction, it could be argued, is devoted to bringing news to the reader of events in this "completely new world." Richard Pevear, one of the translators of an admirable new version of *Crime and Punishment* in English, done with Larissa Volokhonsky, asserts just that in his preface to that translation:

> The ambiguous laughter of this demiurge or demon can be heard in all of Dostoevsky's later works. Here, in germ, was

the reality that challenged his powers of imitation, an indefinite "something new," a completely new and unfamiliar world, prosaic and at the same time fantastic, which could have no image until he gave it one, but was *more real* than the vanishing spectacle he contemplated on the Neva.

ANTHONY TROLLOPE'S DANGEROUS HABIT

Only a few years later, in 1875, on a ship bound from New York to England, the great English novelist, Anthony Trollope (1815–82), began to write *An Autobiography*, published posthumously in 1883. No works could seem more different from Dostoevsky's novels than Trollope's forty-seven novels. Dostoevsky's novels have a hectic, melodramatic intensity. The characters seem always to live in, or to be about to vanish into, that hyperreality Dostoevsky glimpsed in his vision by the Neva. Trollope's novels, on the contrary, present stories of everyday courtship, marriage, and inheritance. These involve what look like ordinary middle- and upper-class Victorian men and women. As Henry James observed in his essay of 1883 on Trollope's work, Trollope's "great, his inestimable merit was a complete appreciation of the usual." After *Barchester Towers* Trollope, says James, "settled down steadily to the English girl; he took possession of her, and turned her inside out . . . he bestowed upon her the most serious, the most patient, the most tender, the most copious consideration."

This formulation makes it look as if Trollope's novels are to be valued for their accuracy of representation, for their truthful correspondence to the social realities of Victorian English middle-class life. Nothing could be further from the case. When the reader enters the world of a given Trollope novel he or she enters a place that is the ordinary, usual, Victorian world transfigured into something uniquely Trollopean. This is evident, for example, in the quite extraordinary assumption, mentioned earlier, that is a law of Trollope's fiction. This is the assumption that people have clairvoyant insight into what other people are thinking and feeling. Trollope's novels are more like science fiction, or even, in their own way, like Dostoevsky's novels, than like what we ordinarily think of as a transcription of reality, things as they are, or were. The multitude of Trollope's characters is each surrounded by his or her own circumambient social world. They are certainly among those who have come alive in my imagination and remain alive for me. Lily Dale, Septimus Harding, and the rest are going on living somewhere in my mind as ghosts or specters. They abide there, waiting to be reinvoked the next time I read the particular novels in which they appear.

Proof of this detachment of Trollope's novels from the "real world" is given in a strange confession Trollope makes early in *An Autobiography*. The passage is a key to understanding his conception of the imaginary, that is, to understanding the mode of existence of his novels. The passage presents Trollope's version of a conviction that literature is a recording not of the real world but of an independently existing imaginary world. In this passage Trollope is speaking of the way he was ostracized as a youth at Harrow because he was a day pupil at an elite boarding school and had little pocket money or good clothes. He says that since play with the other boys was denied him, he had to make up his own solitary play for himself: "Play of some kind was necessary to me then, – as it has always been." Trollope's solitary play took the form of what today we would call "daydreaming":

Thus it came to pass that I was always going about with some castle-in-the-air firmly built within my mind. Nor were these efforts in architecture spasmodic, or subject to constant change from day to day. For weeks, for months, if I remember rightly, from year to year I would carry on the same tale, binding myself down to certain laws, to certain proportions and proprieties and unities. Nothing impossible was ever introduced, – not even anything which from outward circumstances would seem to be violently improbable.

What is a daydream? It would seem to be distinguishable from a real dream. The daydream is quasi-voluntary, while the real dream seems to proceed of its own accord, outside the dreamer's control. Trollope's account seems to agree with this in the way he uses a metaphor of architecture for his daydreams, as if to suggest that they were deliberately constructed. He also indicates that he bound himself down to certain laws, proportions, proprieties, and unities, as though the shape of the daydream were more or less within his control. Things are not quite so simple, however, as anyone who has ever daydreamed (most people, I suppose) will know. Though the daydream seems voluntary enough, or at least half-voluntary, in its origin, once its presuppositions get established it seems to continue more or less of its own accord, as a kind of involuntary wish-fulfillment. The daydream takes on a life of its own.

Trollope's account of his youthful daydreaming is a hyperbolic version of this. Most daydreams are short and intermittent – mine at least. For a brief period I imagine an alternative reality, not a very vivid one, alas. That is why I need to read novels and could not write one. In Trollope's case, however, the same daydream was carried on from week to week, from month to month, even from year to year, like a long-running television serial. Trollope was that reprehensible thing, a day-dreamer, with a vengeance. During all the time of the serial daydream Trollope lived in two worlds. One was the real and not very satisfactory one (for Trollope at that time). The other world was an imaginary one in which the goals were attained that Sigmund Freud ascribed to the virtual world of literature. Freud said art is the attainment in imagination of what all men (sic!) want, that is, honor, wealth, and the love of women, by someone who has been deprived of those in real life. Trollope's continuous daydreaming is an extravagant example of this. He tells the reader just that in his confession:

> I myself was of course my own hero. Such is a necessity of castle-building. But I never became a king, or a duke, – much less, when my height and personal appearance were fixed, would I be an Antinous, or six feet high. I never was a learned man, nor even a philosopher. But I was a very clever person, and beautiful young women used to be fond of me. And I strove to be kind of heart and open of hand and noble in thought, despising mean things, and altogether I was a very much better fellow than I have ever succeeded in being since.

The only parallel I can think of to Trollope's account of his daydreaming habit is one of the stories in The Fifty-Minute Hour: A Collection of True Psychoanalytic Tales (1954). This is a set of narratives, apparently about his patients, told by a practicing psychiatrist, Robert Lindner (1914–56). "The Jet-Propelled Couch" is the story of a high-tech scientist, habitual reader of science fiction, who begins gradually to believe that he is two persons, one the sober scientist doing his (more or less) ordinary, everyday work, the other having all sorts of adventures in outer space. The twist at the end is that the psychiatrist, rather than curing the patient, comes himself to believe in that other world, just as I as a child believed in the metaworld of *The Swiss Family Robinson*, or just as I believe even today in the worlds of Trollope's various novels when I read them. Reading literature might be defined as a way of letting someone else do your daydreaming for you. A crucial difference exists, however, as I shall specify, with Trollope's help.

The young Anthony Trollope's daydreams were remarkably like the grown-up Trollope's novels in one important way at least. They were long continuous stories that strictly obeyed rules of consistency and probability. The reader can count on several reassuring things in any Trollope novel. The characters will go on being consistent with themselves from one end of the novel to the other. The world they dwell in will remain the same too. Moreover, nothing beyond the "usual" will often occur. The "English girl," for the most part, will win her true love and live happily ever after. The exceptions to this are of great interest, just because they are unusual, for example the story of Lily Dale's failure to marry as it is carried on from *The Small House at Allington* to *The Last Chronicle of Barset*.

That Trollope's published novels were a transformation of his youthful habit of daydreaming is made explicit by Trollope himself. Speaking of that bad habit of daydreaming, Trollope says,

> There can, I imagine, hardly be a more dangerous mental practice, but I have often doubted whether, had it not been my practice, I should ever have written a novel. I learned in this way to maintain an interest in a fictitious story, to dwell on a work created by my own imagination, and to live in a world altogether outside the world of my own material life.

By this point, toward the end of the passage I have been

analyzing, Trollope is describing the imaginary universe of his daydreams or of a given novel as having been created, perhaps, by his own imagination, but as then coming to have an independent existence. He can enter into it and dwell within it.

Two crucial differences differentiate Trollope's daydreams from his novels. The daydreams remained private, secret, hidden, solitary. We shall never know anything more about them than the meager generalities he gives in this passage. The novels, on the contrary, were written down and published. This made them accessible to all who choose to read them. A Trollope novel, one might say, is the transcription in words of a "world altogether outside the world of [Trollope's] own material life." In that peculiar way I am attempting to define, the imaginary world is not dependent on words for its existence. It is not brought into existence by words. The novel's words are performative, all right, but their performative function is to give the reader access to a realm that seems to exist apart from the words, even though the reader cannot enter it except by way of the words.

Another difference is equally important. Trollope was his own hero in his youthful daydreams. The novels are about imaginary characters, many of them women. These can only by a series of hypothetical and unverifiable relays be identified with Trollope himself. Trollope says as much at the end of the paragraph: "In after years I have done the same [i.e. dwelled in imaginary worlds], – with this difference, that I have discarded the hero of my early dreams, and have been able to lay my own identity aside." Literature begins, as Kafka asserted, when "Ich" becomes "er," when "I" becomes "he" (or, in Trollope's case, often "she"). That transformation turned Trollope the guilty daydreamer ("There can . . . hardly be a more dangerous mental practice . . .") into Trollope the great and admirably productive novelist.

HENRY JAMES'S UNTRODDEN FIELD OF SNOW

Trollope's novels are radically different from Dostoevsky's. Nevertheless, they unexpectedly have, according to the authors themselves, somewhat similar origins in imaginary worlds outside the real world. Henry James (1843–1916) differs sharply from both these writers in the texture and quality of his fictions. James's work deals with super-subtle nuances of intersubjective interchange between characters who are nothing if not intelligent and sensitive. A whole page, for example, is devoted in The Wings of the Dove to reporting the analysis by one character of the implications of an "Oh!" uttered by another character. Nevertheless, for James too, in an even more surprisingly affirmative way, a literary work does no more than report with more or less accuracy an independently existing hyper-reality.

In the last of the magisterial prefaces James began writing in 1906 for the New York edition of his work, the preface to The Golden Bowl, James discusses his re-reading of his novels and tales. He re-read them not only in order to write the prefaces, but also in order to perform the work of revision to which he subjected some of them. This was especially the case with the earlier works. An example is The Portrait of a Lady, for which he made hundreds of small and large revisions. The Golden Bowl, he reports, did not require any revision. The figures James uses to describe his experiences of re-reading are characteristically extravagant and baroque. The figures define James's sense of the way each work gives access to an independently existing imaginary world, a different one for each work. Re-reading, James says, is re-vision. To re-read is to see again what James calls the "matter of the tale." This "matter" is its basic substance, something independent of the words that record it. The word "matter" was used archaically to name a body of narrative material that might give rise to many different written works. In medieval times one spoke of "the matter of Arthur" or of "the matter of Troy," meaning the whole collection of legends centering on King Arthur or on the Trojan War.

James figures the "matter of the tale" for *The Golden Bowl* as a great expanse of untrodden snow. It is a striking image. The story recorded in *The Golden Bowl* is substantially there. It is a material substrate or "subjectile." This is the odd French word that names the basic surface of underlay, or paper, or plaster on which a painting is applied. The "matter" is a surface on which to write, and, at the same time, that about which the story is written. Jacques Derrida uses the word "subjectile" in the title of his long second essay on Antonin Artaud, "Forcener le subjectile (To Unsense the Subjectile)." He defines "subjectile" as follows:

> The notion belongs to the code of painting and designates what is in some way lying below *(subjectum)* as a substance, a subject, a succubus. Between the beneath and the above, it is at once a support and a surface, sometimes also the matter of a painting or a sculpture, everything distinct from form, as well as from meaning and representation, not representable (ce qui n'est pas représentable).

James's field of snow, the "matter of the tale," is just such a subjectile, though for a novel, not for a painting or a sculpture.

The actual words of a given novel or story James figures as his footsteps on the untrodden, virgin snow. With his earlier works, James says, his feet no longer walk easily in the old footprints, and so he must revise. He finds, he says, in the ponderous manner of his late style (like an elephant stepping delicately), a

> frequent lapse of harmony between my present mode of motion and that to which the existing footprints were due. It was, all sensibly, as if the clear matter being still there, even as a shining expanse of snow spread over a plain, my exploring tread, for application to it, had quite unlearned the old pace and found itself naturally falling into another, which might sometimes indeed more or less agree with the original tracks, but might most often, or very nearly, break the surface in other places.

With his more recent works, *The Golden Bowl*, for example, James says his feet and stride fit perfectly in the old footmarks. In that case, revision does not need to follow "re-vision," the re-reading that leads to a renewed vision of the primary matter of the tale:

> As the historian of the matter sees and speaks, so my intelligence of it, as a reader, meets him half-way, passive, receptive, appreciative, often even grateful, unconscious, quite blissfully, of any bar to intercourse, any disparity of sense between us. Into his very footprints the responsive, the imaginative steps of the docile reader that I consentingly become for him all comfortably sink. His vision, superimposed on my own as an image in cut paper is applied to a sharp shadow on a wall, matches, at every point, without excess or deficiency.

This does not mean that the account of that particular tale's matter James gave in *The Golden Bowl* was any more adequate than was the correspondence of *The Portrait of a Lady* to its matter. This inadequacy holds in both cases, even though the latter was substantially revised for the New York Edition, while the former was not. How could tracks in a feature-less expanse of snow adequately represent that snow? The "matter" is undifferentiated. It is a kind of nothing, incommensurate with any differentiation, such as words necessarily provide. James's satisfaction with *The Golden Bowl* means only that he has not yet changed enough to be led to give a different account of this particular matter.

The "historian of the matter" is the narrator James had originally invented to tell the tale. To speak of him as a "historian," however, is to imply the independent existence of the matter of the tale. James has not made it up. It is *there*, always already, waiting for its historian. It would remain there, latent subjectile, empty plain of fresh snow, waiting for its historian, even if no historian were ever to show up.

Once more it is the independent, pre-existing "being there" of the alternative world to which James in his own way testifies. The reader has access to that alternative world only through the words James has written, the footsteps he has inscribed on the snow. Or, to use the alternative figure he employs, we can know only the silhouette James has cut out. This fits more or less well within the shadow on the wall, but only James can see the latter. James has the unique privilege of having direct access to the subjectile, the prime matter of the tale. This privilege lives and dies with him. It is a privilege not available to any other reader. James alone is able to set the cut-out silhouette against the shadow on the wall. This allows him, uniquely, to measure the adequacy, the fullness and accuracy, of the "historian's" report.

The most instructive cases, James reports, are those in which his new footsteps do not fit the old. They are most instructive because they make salient the independent existence of the matter. That in turn leads to a clear experience of the coercive power the matter has. The new footsteps are not a matter of choice. They are demanded of him, by an irresistible coercion, through a re-reading that is a return to the latent matter of the story:

> What was thus predominantly interesting to note, at all events, was the high spontaneity of these deviations and differences, which became thus things not of choice, but of immediate and perfect necessity: necessity to the end of dealing with the quantities in question at all.

The irresistible enchantment of the "old matter" issues on a re-reading a renewed demand that cannot be evaded. This is a demand for responsible response and acknowledgment. The demand is renewed, that is, as a need to add more words to the old words. This urgent need is figured by James, in an obscurely sexual figure, as the "perforation" of "more adequate channels." This perhaps justifies my use of the term "virgin" for that snow.

One form this renewed response takes is the prefaces themselves. They are, taken together, no doubt the greatest treatise in English on the art of the novel. The prefaces are so powerful and beguiling, even if sometimes so misleading, that it is difficult, once you have read them, to read James's work in any way other than the way the prefaces direct the reader to do it. That latent matter seems to make an insatiable demand for more language, more commentary. One evidence of this is the exorbitance of the prefaces. They often end by saying something like the following (to cite the end of the preface to *The Portrait of a Lady*): "There is really too much to say." The renewed stream of words is generated by an act of faith, almost of religious belief. This act of faith requires new testimony to that belief:

> The "old" matter is there, re-accepted, re-tasted, exquisitely re-assimilated and re-enjoyed – believed in, to be brief, with the same "old" grateful faith . . . ; and yet for due testimony, for re-assertion of value, perforating, as by some strange and fine, some latent and gathered force, a myriad more adequate channels.

James's expression of what it is like to re-appropriate the old matter through an act of re-reading is characteristically extravagant:

> No march, accordingly, I was soon enough aware, could possibly be more confident and free than this infinitely interesting and amusing *act* of re-appropriation; shaking off all shackles of theory, unattended, as was speedily to appear, with humiliating uncertainties, and almost as enlivening, or at least as momentous, as, to a philosophic mind, a sudden large apprehension of the Absolute. What indeed could be more delightful than to enjoy a sense of the absolute in such easy conditions?

"A sudden large apprehension of the Absolute!" That is certainly a hyperbolic description, to say the least, of a simple act of re-reading one of one's earlier works, noting the way one would write it differently now, and by that act re-appropriating the source matter on which the work was based.

Why does James call what is apprehended in this nota-tion of difference, "the Absolute?" The word "absolute" means, etymologically, untied, free of all distinctions, dif-ferentiations, and self-divisions. The word has Hegelian connotations. It is Hegel's name for the end of history. When that end is reached the long dialectical process will be complete. All divisions between self and other will be transcended in an ultimate *Aufhebung* or sublation. The wide plain of untrodden snow that figures the matter of the tale is a good image for this sort of Absolute. James's term "the Absolute" confirms my claim that for James the matter of the tale both demands all the details and subtleties of a novel like *The Golden Bowl*, and at the same time is, in itself, strangely featureless. It is undifferentiated, a kind of emptiness. It is in short, like the Absolute figured as a field of untrodden snow.

James's formulations stress the pleasure of this apprehension of the Absolute. It is entirely spontaneous, free of all shackles. It is free, for example, of encumbrance by the deliberate labor of theoretical reflection. It is also free of any humiliating uncertainties, such as uncertainty about the adequacy of one's account in words of the matter in question. It is "confident," "free," "infinitely interesting and amusing," "enlivening." To apprehend the Absolute directly, without mediation, in the strange form of an experienced deviation between how James wrote it then and how he would write it now is the source, it is clear from James's description, of an intense pleasure. This pleasure is by no means simply that of an increase in knowledge. It is bodily, even sensuous. It is quasi-sexual in its affective intensity.

WALTER BENJAMIN'S "PURE LANGUAGE"

An analogous passage is a celebrated account by Walter Benjamin (1892–1940) of what happens when one notes the discrepancy between source text and translation. The passage is in Benjamin's "The Task of the Translator." In Henry James's case, the revision of an earlier work is imperiously demanded of him by a new apprehension of its originating matter. This rewriting is like a translation of that work into a new language. Just as, for James, the difference between old version and new allows an apprehension of the Absolute, so Benjamin's account of the relation of a translation to its original affirms that the discrepancies between the two allow a glimpse of a "pure language (reine Sprache)." That pure language is the origin of both. At the same time, in its "absolute" purity, this pure language is the disqualification of both original and translation. I am citing, the reader will note, a translation of Benjamin's essay. The difficulties of translating that essay exemplify the issues of translation the essay is about.

In a powerful, though by no means entirely perspicuous figure, Benjamin compares the original and the translation to adjacent pieces of a broken pot. These need not be similar but must fit together in order to reassemble the whole vessel:

> Fragments of a vessel which are to be glued together must match one another in the smallest details, although they need not be like one another. In the same way a translation, instead of resembling the meaning of the original, must lovingly and in detail incorporate the original's mode of signification, thus making both the original and the translation recognizable as fragments of a greater language, just as fragments are part of a vessel.

The difficulty here is making the phrase: "the original's mode of signification" match the assertion that original and translation must fit one another like adjacent fragments of a broken pot. How are those jagged edges like the original's mode of signification? What, the reader might in addition ask, is the force of that "in the same way"? This phrase translates "so" in the German original. "So" in German is not too far from the English "so," but has a slightly different range of meanings. "So" in German means "so, thus; like this or that," as an adverb, and "so, therefore, consequently," as a conjunction. Here is an example of translation problems that arise with the simplest word. The figure of the broken pot translates into an image the relation of original and translation that is in question here. "In the same way," "so" names the relation of similarity and difference between the literal subject and the figure Benjamin invents as the only adequate way to express it.

A "greater language," exceeding both original and translation, is figured by Benjamin as the whole vessel, of which both original and translation are adjacent fragments, "in the same way" as James's two sets of footprints across the snow-covered plain by no means cover the whole matter of the tale. What Benjamin means by the "whole vessel" is made more explicit in a remarkable sentence a couple of paragraphs further in the essay. The "greater language" is that "pure language" that encompasses both original and translation, and of which they give news, though always inadequate news. The greater language is in itself "pure," in the sense of being undifferentiated, therefore empty, meaningless, since meaning depends on differentiation. The origin of language and meaning is itself without meaning, like James's Absolute. "In this pure language," writes Benjamin, or rather writes his translator, "– which no longer means or expresses anything but is, as expressionless and creative Word, that which is meant in all languages – all information, all sense, and all intention finally encounter a stratum in which they are destined to be extinguished."

LITERATURE AS LIE IN PROUST

Work by Marcel Proust (1871–1922) differs greatly from the work of Dostoevsky, Trollope, James, or Benjamin. The title of Proust's immense pseudo-autobiographical novel, *À la recherche du temps perdu*, is traditionally translated as *Remembrance of Things Past*, a phrase from Shakespeare. The English title misses the quasi-scientific connotation of "recherche." The work is a research into the possibility of finding lost time. One recurrent motif in Proust's *Recherche* is the idea that artworks – painting, music, or literature – hint that there must be an immense proliferation of possible alternative worlds. Only some of these have actually been translated into paint, sounds, or words. Proust, or rather his imaginary protagonist and narrator, whom the latter at one point says you may call "Marcel," affirms that a different virtual reality exists for each artist. This differs from my claim that each work, even those by the same author, opens up a different world.

Proust, moreover, makes explicit, as my other authorities do not, the connection of the artwork with lies. Nothing could be more traditional than to associate poetry with lying. Sir Philip Sydney explicitly does this, for example, in *An Apology for Poetry* (1595). Sydney there claims that the poet does not lie because he (!) does not claim to be telling the truth: "he nothing affirms, and therefore never lieth." That is a way of admitting that if you are taken in by poetry, it acts like a lie that is believed. An example would be the "Preface" to *Robinson Crusoe*, in which Defoe claims to be no more than the editor of truthful memoirs: "The editor believes the thing to be a just history of fact; neither is there any appearance of fiction in it." Both parts of this sentence are lies. They will beguile an unwary reader who does not happen to know that they are part of the fiction.

Literature is like lying in that both a literary work and a lie are contrary to fact statements, with no corresponding referent. They are also alike in that both can be performatively felicitous if they are believed in. If I say "It's pouring rain" when it is a sunny day, and that persuades you to put on your raincoat, my statement is false but is nevertheless an efficacious speech act. The opening of _The Wings of the Dove_ ("She waited, Kate Croy, for her father to come in . . . ") is a lie. This is the case in the sense that in the "real world" there never was a Kate Croy who waited for her father. If the words work, however, to give the reader, at least the one who grants them credence, access to the imaginary world of _The Wings of the Dove_, then those opening words are, constatively, a lie, but, performatively, "felicitous," to use J. L. Austin's term in _How To Do Things with Words_, still the classic book on speech act theory. James's words work, happily, to make something happen.

Proust implicitly asserts the similarity of lies and literature by saying the same things about both. In a passage about the way the writer Bergotte (a fictitious writer in the novel) always chooses as mistresses women who lie to him and whose lies he believes, Marcel, in an eloquent formulation, generalizes about the power lies have, if we believe in them, to open doors to worlds we otherwise never would have known. The anacoluthonic shift from singular third person, "he" (speaking about Bergotte), to first person plural, "we" (speaking about the narrator's own lies, for example those he tells his mistress Albertine), implicitly generalizes the power lies have. Lies anyone tells, if they are believed, are efficacious. Other examples are the lies Albertine tells Marcel, detailed at great length elsewhere in the _Recherche_:

The lie, the perfect lie, about people we know, about the

relations we have had with them, about our motive for some action, formulated by us in totally different terms, the lie as to what we are, whom we love, what we feel with regard to people who love us and believe that they have fashioned us in their own image because they keep on kissing us morning, noon, and night – that lie is one of the few things in the world that can open windows for us on to what is new and unknown, that can awaken in us sleeping senses for the contemplation of universes that otherwise we should never have known.

No doubt this passage in one of its dimensions refers cryptically to Marcel Proust's own lies in inventing a "straight" protagonist who nevertheless covertly and indirectly expresses the author's homosexuality. An example is the way the names of the chief women in Marcel's life are feminized masculine names: Gilberte, Albertine, Andrée.

In a later passage Marcel says more or less the same thing about artworks, including literary ones, as he says about lies. The context is his hearing a performance of the posthumous septet by the fictitious composer in the *Recherche*, Vinteuil. The score has been laboriously deciphered after Vinteuil's death from notations that are as obscure, Marcel says, as cuneiform writing. As he listens to the septet, Marcel recognizes its similarity to other work by Vinteuil. He derives from that recognition the notion that each artist brings us news of a virtual reality that we have no other way to know: "Each artist seems thus to be the native of an unknown country, which he himself has forgotten, and which is different from that whence another great artist, setting sail for the earth (appareillant pour la terre), will eventually emerge." Marcel affirms that "composers do not actually remember this lost fatherland, but each of them remains all his life unconsciously attuned to it; he is delirious with joy when he sings in harmony with his native land." If Vinteuil's cryptic notes had never been deciphered we should never have had access to his "lost fatherland," just as we would never have known the separate universe of Victor Hugo's *Légende des Siècles* or his *Contemplations* if Hugo had died before writing them, nor the world of Proust's *Recherche* if he had died in 1910: "What is to us his [Vinteuil's] real achievement would have remained purely potential (virtuel), as unknown as those universes to which our perception does not reach, of which we shall never have any idea."

For Proust, as you can see, those innumerable alternative universes always already exist, virtually. They are discovered by artists, musicians, and writers, not invented by them. Some of those possible realities are brought into our everyday world by paintings, music, or literature. Those universes would, however, go on existing even if every copy of Hugo's *Contemplations*, Proust's *Recherche*, or Vinteuil's septet were destroyed. Luckily for us, these works and others like them exist and give us access to a kind of perpetually flowing fountain of youth. The treasure of artworks allows us to multiply and diversify our lives immeasurably. "The only true voyage of discovery," says Marcel,

> the only really rejuvenating experience (le seul bain de Jouvence: literally "the only fountain of youth"), would be . . . to see the universe through the eyes of another, of a hundred others, to see the hundred universes that each of them sees, that each of them is; and this we can do with an Elstir [the painter in the *Recherche*], with a Vinteuil.

MAURICE BLANCHOT'S SIRENS' SONG

Maurice Blanchot is without doubt one of the greatest of twentieth-century literary critics. His essays discuss a multitude of writers, including James and Melville among American authors. At the same time, Blanchot's essays are a constantly renewed, endlessly mediated, investigation of the question "What is literature?" Blanchot's most important essay on Proust is called "The Experience of Proust." That essay is the second half of a long essay called "The Song of the Sirens: Encountering the Imaginary." "The Song of the Sirens" is the opening essay of *Le livre à venir* (*The Book To Come*), one collection of Blanchot's essays. Blanchot's reading of Proust is congruent with mine in distinguishing between two experiences of time in Proust. One is the famous transcendence of time in a co-presence of two times at the end of the novel. In that climactic episode Marcel re-experiences the sensation of uneven paving stones before St. Mark's in Venice when he steps again on uneven paving stones at the entrance to the Guermantes' house in Paris, many years later. Past time seems to be recaptured.

Blanchot, however, correctly sees this experience of recovering lost time as misleading many readers and critics. The real "experience of Proust" is what Blanchot calls "un peu de temps à l'état pur," a fragment of time in a pure state. This pure time Blanchot sees as the time out of time, that "other time," the time of the "image":

> Yes, in this time, everything becomes image, and the essence of the image is to be completely exterior, without intimacy, and nevertheless more inaccessible and more mysterious than the thinking in the interior of the self; without significance, but calling toward the depths of every possible

meaning; unrevealed and nevertheless manifest, having that presence-absence which constitutes the drawing power and fascination of the Sirens.

This other time is, for Blanchot, the origin of writing. It is "the secret of writing." This pure time commands the transformation of all Marcel's worldly experience into that imaginary space where everything becomes image. What is essential for Proust, Blanchot asserts, is

that revelation by which, in a single blow, as well as also, nevertheless, little by little, by that grasp of another time, he is introduced into the transformed intimacy of time, there where he has at his disposal a pure time, serving as a principle of metamorphosis and of the imaginary as well as of a space which is already the reality of the power to write.

Another time, a "pure time," like Benjamin's "pure speech" that is a single all-embracing senseless word; a space of the imaginary that is a place of constant metamorphosis, little by little and yet all at once – these are the basic features Blanchot ascribes to Proust's "secret of writing." The first part of "The Song of the Sirens" uses the story of Ulysses's encounter with the Sirens as an extended allegory defining more generally "the encounter with the imaginary." More precisely, it is an allegory that is not an allegory, but the literal truth. Somewhat surprisingly (given what we ordinarily think of James and Blanchot), the version of my concept of literature that is closest to Blanchot's, among those so far discussed, is James's notion of the "clear matter of the tale" as a featureless expanse of snow. Benjamin's idea of "pure speech" is also close to Blanchot's "pure time." Most of the other writers I have discussed in this chapter, and I too, think of the actual literary work, the words on the page, as the material embodiment of events that exist in some imaginary realm in all their richness of detail, waiting, perhaps indefinitely, to be incarnated in words. That was my spontaneous belief about *The Swiss Family Robinson*.

For Blanchot, however, somewhat as for James, the realm of the imaginary, though it is the origin of all the richness and complexity of the literary work, is itself featureless, empty, an abyss. The story of Ulysses and the Sirens expresses this. Or rather, the story is itself the experience of that contradictory origin. As in the case of Blanchot's discussion of Proust, his reading of the Sirens episode in the *Odyssey* depends on a distinction between two kinds of time. The reader will remember that Ulysses had been warned by Circe that he and his shipmates would encounter the two Sirens. They come as doubles, like the many sinister doubles in Kafka's *The Trial*. One would be more than enough. Two is too many, a kind of uncanny, disturbing, self-reflecting, mirroring duplicity. Freud in "The Uncanny" names the doubling of persons as one version of the uncanny. Especially uncanny is to meet one's own double face to face, as the Sirens do all the time, or as twins perhaps do.

Circe told Ulysses to stop the other mariners' ears with wax. She said he should order them to tie him to the mast so he could hear their song and yet not be able to yield to it, as his ship was rowed safely by the Sirens' island. The words Ulysses heard are recorded by Homer, though not of course the melody. What he hears, however, is a preliminary song that promises a real song. That real song will come later if Ulysses and his men go ashore. The Sirens' song is always proleptic, a beckoning toward the future. "Draw near," they sing,

illustrious Odysseus, flower of Achaean chivalry, and bring
your ship to rest so that you may hear our voices. No seaman
ever sailed his black ship past this spot without listening to
the sweet tones that flow from our lips, and none that listened
has not been delighted and gone on a wiser man.

As Circe has forewarned Ulysses, if they go ashore, he and his
men will join the mouldering and bleached bones of the
Sirens' previous victims.

Blanchot's essay begins by noting that what the Sirens sing
to Ulysses is, as I have said earlier here, not their real song but
the promise of a song to come. Blanchot goes beyond
Homer's text, however, to a reading of it that sees the Sirens'
song as an embodiment of literature in its relation to an origin that is always ahead, behind, or elsewhere, never present
as such. That is what is unsatisfying about the Sirens' song:

The Sirens: evidently they really sang, but in a way that was
not satisfying, that only implied in which direction lay the true
sources of the song, the true happiness of the song.
Nevertheless, through their imperfect songs, songs which
were only a singing still to come, they guided the sailor
toward that space where singing would really begin.

The problem is that the place which is the true origin of
song, where the song really begins, is also the place where
singing stops. In a somewhat similar way, all meaning vanishes
in the pure speech or wordless Word that Walter Benjamin
hypothesizes as the meaning of both original and translation:

What was that place? It was a place where the only thing left
was to disappear, because in this region of source and origin,
music itself had disappeared more completely than in any

other place in the world; it was like a sea into which the living would sink with their ears closed and where the Sirens, too, even they, as proof of their good will, would one day have to disappear.

The origin of song, for Blanchot, the reader can see, is a blank and ominous silence. It is the silence of a sea that has closed over someone who has sunk beneath its surface, or it is the silence of a trackless and dessicated desert:

> . . . that beyond was only a desert, . . . the region where music originated was the only place completely without music, a sterile dry place where silence, like noise, buried all access to the song in anyone who had once had command of it.

Blanchot distinguishes between two kinds of literature in terms of their relation to this silent origin of song. One is the novel, inaugurated, Blanchot implies, in the *Odyssey*, with its tale of the wily Ulysses who comes to the Isle of the Sirens unscathed from earlier adventures. Ulysses cleverly figures out a way to hear the Sirens and not to succumb to them, to get off scot-free. He can then go on to still further adventures that will lead him ultimately back into the arms of Penelope and into old age as a good family man. Blanchot does not greatly admire either the novel or Ulysses, to put it mildly. He sees novels as secretly motivated by their desire to suppress, ignore, cover over, and forget the encounter with the imaginary that is their secret origin. This makes the novel "the most attractive of genres, the one which, in its discretion and its cheerful nothingness, takes upon itself the task of forgetting what others degrade by calling it the essential." Blanchot means, I suppose, that the "secret of literature" is more than essential. It is a sort of hyperbolic essential, the essential cubed.

Récit - a brief novel, simple, narrative line, 1-st person narrator

Opposed to the novel is the récit, which Lydia Davis somewhat misleadingly translates as the "tale." A récit, for example those remarkable récits by Blanchot himself, Death Sentence, The Madness of the Day, and others, takes the encounter with the imaginary as its direct focus. The story of Ulysses and the Sirens is a récit buried within the generally novelistic Odyssey. Blanchot's other example of a récit in this essay is, somewhat surprisingly, given the usual brevity of the récit, that monster anti-novel, Melville's Moby Dick. This juxtaposition suggests that there are two possible outcomes for a récit: the death of the protagonist as he is swallowed up in the imaginary, in the image, in the originary silence (Ahab in Moby Dick), or the survival of the protagonist in a refusal and forgetting (Ulysses in the Odyssey).

Though Blanchot does not say so in this essay, more commonly in a récit, even in his own, there are two protagonists, one who dies and one who survives to tell the tale. Marlow, for example, survives the death of Kurtz in Conrad's Heart of Darkness. Ishmael, Melville's first-person narrator in Moby Dick, survives the death of Ahab and the sinking of the Pequod. He is left floating on Queequeg's coffin to be able to tell the tale we have been reading. The storyteller is a survivor. If there is to be a story, there must be someone left to tell the tale. Conrad's Marlow eloquently formulates this relation between the one who crosses over into "the invisible" and the one who survives:

> And it is not my own extremity I remember best – a vision of greyness without form filled with physical pain, and a careless contempt for the evanescence of all things – even of this pain itself. No! It is his [Kurtz's] extremity that I seem to have lived through. True, he had made that last stride, he had stepped

over the edge, while I had been permitted to draw back my hesitating foot. And perhaps in this is the whole difference; perhaps all the wisdom, and all truth, and all sincerity, are just compressed into that inappreciable moment of time in which we step over the threshold of the invisible. Perhaps!

Conrad must say "perhaps," because how would you know one way or the other without stepping over that threshold yourself? Dead men, as we know, tell no tales, and no one can die the death of another.

Blanchot's *Death Sentence* is told by the survivor of another's death. The narrator of *The Madness of the Day* is his own survivor, the survivor of a trauma that gave him blinding insight. All Blanchot's work as a critic is written, it might be said, by someone who has survived his own death. Blanchot the critic combines both protagonists of *Death Sentence* in one, just as Ulysses does by being the only man who has heard the Sirens sing and has nevertheless survived. To show just how that is so, however, would take me too far afield, for example into a reading of that extraordinary late quasi-autobiographical work by Blanchot, *The Instant of My Death* (1994). This small *récit* tells the tale of how someone, a "he," perhaps Maurice Blanchot himself, survived the experience of being face to face with a Nazi firing squad during the German occupation of France in World War II.

One more "essential" point must be made about what Blanchot says in "The Song of the Sirens" about "the secret of writing." I have said that the story of Ulysses and the Sirens is not an allegorical representation of literature's relation to its origin. "This is not an allegory," insists Blanchot. Why not? The answer is that the words on the page are not an indirect report of the space of the imaginary, that space where everything has become image. The words on the page are not a way of speaking otherwise, that is, of speaking exoterically about something "secret" and perpetually esoteric. That would be allegory proper. No, the words on the page as they are formed by the hand of the writer or as they are read, one by one, by the reader, are the temporal movement whereby that origin, so it seems, comes into existence. The point of origin, in a paradoxical combination of creation and discovery that I have named already, is both brought into being by the words of the *récit* and, at the same time, it is discovered, uncovered, revealed as something that was always already there. "The tale," says Blanchot, in an elegant formulation of this paradox that is the true "secret of writing,"

> is a movement towards a point, a point which is not only unknown, obscure, foreign, but such that apart from this movement, it does not seem to have any sort of real prior existence, and yet it is so imperious that the tale derives its power of attraction only from this point, so that it cannot even "begin" before reaching it – and yet only the tale and the unpredictable movement of the tale create the space where the point becomes real, powerful, and alluring.

A key word in this long sentence is "movement," three times repeated. "Movement" names at once the spatial movement from word to word across the page and the movement of the protagonist from one experience to another. It names also the incessant movement of time as it goes forward toward an ever-unattainable future goal. That goal turns out always to belong also to an immemorial past, to that "other time" or "time without time" with which Blanchot's essays and his *récits* are obsessively concerned.

An example of this obsession is Blanchot's striking description, from a much later essay than "The Song of the Sirens," of a perpetual march without getting anywhere, across the desert space of the imaginary. Blanchot ascribes this march to Melville's Bartleby in "Bartleby the Scrivener." In Blanchot's reading of Bartleby's "I would prefer not to," Bartleby becomes doubled and doubled again into a whole army of "destroyed men." Bartleby's "I would prefer not to . . . ," says Blanchot, "belongs to the infiniteness of patience; no dialectical intervention can take hold of such passivity. We have fallen out of being, outside where, immobile, proceeding with a slow and even step, destroyed men come and go."

LITERATURE AS THE WHOLLY OTHER: JACQUES DERRIDA

My last ally in my claim that literary works refer not to the real world but to an independently existing alternative world is Jacques Derrida (1930–). Derrida admires Blanchot's work so much and has written so eloquently about Blanchot in so many essays that one might expect him to be close to Blanchot in his concept of literature. "Blanchot," says Derrida, "waits for us still to come, to be read and re-read . . . I would say that never as much as today have I pictured him so far ahead of us." Derrida's most direct answers to the question, "What is literature?" are, however, somewhat surprisingly, derived far more from Edmund Husserl, the father of modern phenomenology, than from Blanchot. Derrida's conception of literature is also one of the relatively few places where he overtly appropriates something from Jean-Paul Sartre.

Derrida's most explicit definitions of literature are given:

(1) in the presentation he made at his thesis defense for his

belatedly taken doctorate at the Sorbonne: "The Time of a Thesis, Punctuations";

(2) in an essay entitled "Passions";

(3) in "Psyché: l'invention de l'autre";

(4) in an interview he gave to Derek Attridge for the opening section of the latter's compilation of essays on literature by Derrida in *Acts of Literature*.

I shall cite and discuss only two passages, one from "The Time of a Thesis," one from "Psyche: Invention of the Other." These two formulations most explicitly align Derrida's definition of literature to the notion I am affirming in this book that a literary work responds to or records a pre-existing perdurable alternative world.

In "The Time of a Thesis" Derrida told his audience at his doctoral defense that his first and most abiding interest had always been in literature. This interest, he said, had come even before his philosophical interest. To confirm this, he asserted that in 1957, many years before he took his doctorate on the basis of his various writings on Hegel, he had "registered," as they say in France, a thesis on "The ideality of the literary object."

Though Derrida never wrote that thesis, it can be said that everything he has written on literature has been directed toward fulfilling that project. All his essays and books on literature, taken together, have made him one of the greatest literary critics and literary theorists of the twentieth century.

What in the world does that mean: "the ideality of the literary object?" A sentence from "The Time of a Thesis" gives the clue. "It was then for me a matter," says Derrida,

of bending, more or less violently, the techniques of transcendental phenomenology to the needs of elaborating a new theory of literature, of that very peculiar type of ideal object that is the literary object, a bound ideality Husserl would have said, bound to so-called "natural" language, a non-mathematical or non-mathematizable object, and yet one that differs from the objects of plastic or musical art, that is to say from all of the examples privileged by Husserl in his analyses of ideal objectivity.

To speak of "the literary object" is to assimilate the literary work to the Husserlian or, more generally, phenomenological, theory of the object. An object is anything that can be "intended" by consciousness, in the peculiar Husserlian sense of "intention." "Intention" means for Husserl the orientation of consciousness toward something or other. Consciousness is always, for the phenomenologists, consciousness of something or other. There is no such thing as empty or naked consciousness. Among all the innumerable objects that consciousness can be conscious of are literary ones.

What does Derrida mean by speaking, in Husserlian terminology, of a literary work as an "ideal object?" This may most easily be explained by an example drawn from geometry. One of Derrida's earliest books was a translation of Husserl's *The Origin of Geometry*, with a long introductory essay by Derrida himself. The triangle is an ideal object in the sense that the triangle would exist even if every triangle drawn on paper or otherwise embodied, even triangles made by the accidental crossing of tree branches, were to be destroyed.

Derrida in his unwritten thesis would have conceded that a literary work is bound to a particular natural language. This means that a translation traduces it, whereas mathematizable ideal objects are, in principle, universal, not dependent on

defame

any "natural language." This, by the way, is a somewhat problematic assumption, to say the least. In spite of conceding the difference between literature and mathematics, Derrida would nevertheless have argued that the ideal literary object "intended" by the reader's consciousness, when he or she reads Proust's *À la recherche du temps perdu* or Dickens's *Great Expectations*, would exist even if every copy of those works were destroyed. Those literary objects would exist even if Proust or Dickens had not written down the works in the first place. Once more we encounter the odd and strongly counter-intuitive notion, present in my childhood experience of *The Swiss Family Robinson*, that the words of a literary work do not create the world they report, but only discover it, or uncover it, for the reader.

Derrida's "Psyche: Invention of the Other" is a reading of a short poem by Francis Ponge. It was written at more or less the same time as "The Time of a Thesis." It confirms Derrida's commitment to the concept of literature in the latter by claiming that a literary work is not "invention" in the sense of making up, fabricating, but in the alternative, more archaic meaning of finding, coming upon. What the writer invents, in the sense of finding or discovering it, is defined by Derrida as the absolutely "other." The literary work as the recording in words of an ideal object "cannot be invented," says Derrida, "except by way of the other, by way of the coming of the other who says 'come' and to which the response of another 'come' appears to be the sole invention that is desirable and worthy of interest." The author of a literary work writes that work in response to an implacable obligation imposed on him or her to turn "the matter of the tale," in Henry James's phrase, into that other strange non-material materiality: words.

A MOTLEY CREW

Dostoevsky, James, Trollope, Proust, Blanchot, Derrida – this is certainly a motley crew! All, however, in quite different ways, support my claim that each literary work gives news of a different and unique alternative reality, a hyper-reality. This reality does not appear to depend on the words of the work for its existence. It seems to be discovered, not fabricated. No way exists to be sure whether or not this is the case. This does not mean, as I have insisted, that literary works are not tied to the real world. They use by displacement words that refer to social, psychological, historical, and physical reality to name the hyper-realities they invent or discover. Reading them, as I have said, is a way of being in the material world. Literary works then re-enter the "real world" in the effects, often decisive, they have on the belief and behavior of those who read them.

Four

VIRTUAL REALITIES ARE GOOD FOR YOU

As I have said, the notion that literature gives access to a virtual reality not otherwise knowable does not have much currency these days. It will seem a bizarre, absurd, or mystified idea to many or to most. It will seem absurd, that is, except to someone who happens to have an unusual gift for reflecting on what happens when he or she reads a literary work. Nor would this concept of literature seem, to most people these days, a sufficient justification for reading works said to be literature. Nevertheless, I claim that this is reason enough. Human beings not only have a propensity to dwell in imaginary worlds. They have a positive need to do so. This need is not in itself unhealthy.

The power of those metaworlds to determine action and judgment in the "real" world, however, sometimes bad action and bad judgment, should not be underestimated. The need to enter some virtual reality will be satisfied in one way or another – if not by literary works, then by computer games, or by films, or by popular songs in video format. It is difficult to imagine a human culture that would not have story-telling or song in some medium or other, oral, handwritten, printed, cinematic, or digital. What we call literature in the modern Western sense of the word just happens to be an important form of the imaginary. It was a form developed during the relatively brief historical period of a predominantly paper culture.

This answer to the question "Why read literature?" satisfies me. It corresponds to my lifelong sense of what literature is and why it is good to read it. Nevertheless, many other quite different and quite incongruous answers to the question of why we should read (or not read) literature have been given during the course of Western history. Often these are present as convictions in the same person or at the same historical moment in a given culture. They have co-existed in an incoherent profusion that never seems to have bothered people much. Literature has been in one way or another granted great authority in the West. It has not seemed absurd to act, decide, or judge "on the authority of literature." Who or what has granted that authority or has been seen as its source?

THE BIBLE IS NOT LITERATURE

Like most aspects of Western culture, the forms of authority granted to literature descend from the Greeks and from the Bible. This heritage has been passed on to us today, with many twists, turns, and permutations through the centuries. This heritage is still "ours," if we belong to Western culture in one of its many current forms. This is so even though "literature" in our current sense is a modern invention, arising with print culture.

It should be remembered, however, that Plato (c. 427–348 BC), Aristotle (384–22 BC), and the Bible are not absolute beginnings. They contain within themselves bits and pieces of far older ideas, stories, and assumptions. The late Victorian writer Walter Pater speaks in *Plato and Platonism* of this aspect of Plato by way of four beautiful figures. Plato's writings are like

a stone that contains fossils within itself, or like a palimpsest, *manuscript*
that is, a manuscript erased and written over that yet contains
the old inscription faintly visible beneath the new, or like a
tapestry woven of threads used before, or like an organic body
that renews itself over time:

> Some of the results of patient earlier thinkers, even then dead
> and gone, are of the structure of his philosophy. They are
> everywhere in it, not as the stray carved corner of some older
> edifice, to be found here or there amid the new, but rather like
> minute relics of earlier organic life in the very stone he builds
> with . . . It is hardly an exaggeration to say that in Plato, in
> spite of his wonderful savour of literary freshness, there is
> nothing absolutely new: or rather, as in many other very
> original products of human genius, the seemingly new is
> old also, a palimpsest, a tapestry of which the actual
> threads have served before, or like the animal frame itself,
> every particle of which has already lived and died many
> times over.

What Pater says of Plato is just as true of the Bible. The Bible
is a sedimented or agglomerate text if there ever was one. It
contains many layers of somewhat heterogeneous accretions.
What justifies my return to the Bible, to Plato, and to Aristotle
here, however, is the way all our modern notions of literature's function are reweavings of themes already present in
these "origins" that are not themselves original.

I would hesitate to speak of the Bible as literature. The
authority it has been granted as the word of God has far
greater force than the authority accorded to secular literature
in our culture, great as the latter has been. The reasons to read
(or not to read) the story of Abraham and Isaac in Genesis
are quite different from the reasons to read (or not to read)

Dickens, Wordsworth, Shakespeare, or even Dante and Milton, religious poets though these latter two are. The demands made on the reader by sacred and secular texts are quite different from one another. Nevertheless, the Bible has been for us the model Book. Different versions of it have been the basic texts for two of the three great "religions of the Book": Judaism and Christianity, just as the Koran is the sacred book for Islam. The expansion of Christianity into a world religion depended on making widely available cheap printed versions of the Christian Bible. The Bible was translated into almost every language under the sun. Protestantism, like modern secular literature, is a concomitant of print culture. It is also a concomitant of Western imperialism. Trade followed the flag, but the flag frequently followed the missionaries who had gone to Christianize foreign lands. The missionaries had often been there first.

The Bible, along with Greek literature, has provided models for most of the genres of secular Western literature: lyric poetry in Psalms, epic or at least "little epic," epyllion, in Job; visionary prophecy in Isaiah, Jeremiah, or Ezekiel, not to speak of those minor prophets, from Daniel and Hosea all the way down to Zecchariah and Malachi; history or chronicle in first and second Chronicles and first and second Kings; narrative in Ruth or Esther, along with all the wonderful models of storytelling in Genesis and Exodus; proverbs in Proverbs; parables in the parables of Jesus in the Gospels; biography in the Gospels; the letter as a form of literature in the epistles of Paul in the New Testament. No doubt it is a long way from St. Paul to Samuel Richardson's *Clarissa*, but the great European epistolary novels of the seventeenth and eighteenth century, by Richardson (1689–1761), Aphra Behn (1640–89), Choderos de Laclos (1741–1803) and many others, find precedents not only in earlier published volumes of "real letters" by distinguished people, but also in the Pauline letters in the New Testament, or in those by James, Peter, John, and Jude. New Testament letters were written to specific addressees, either to collectivities (the Romans, the Philippians, the Corinthians, the Hebrews, and so on) or to specific persons (Gaius in the case of the Third Epistle of John). At the same time they are eventually published and made available to all mankind. One does not have to be a Roman to read Paul's letter to the Romans. In a similar way the reader is given magical access to the private letters of Pamela in Richardson's *Pamela* or of Valmont in *Les liaisons dangereuses*.

The Bible was for millions of people over the generations after the first printed Bible (1535) the basic household "literature" in the more archaic sense of "letters" generally. John Ruskin was still one of those in the nineteenth century who read the Bible systematically through from one end to the other every year. He started again at the beginning, I suppose, on each January 1. The Bible, for Christians in our culture, has absolute authority as God's word. That word was dictated to various inspired scribes and prophetic mediums. It was canonized by the highest church and state authorities. The King James Bible (1611) is so-called because it was redacted under James I's authority. The "Authorized Version" was "appointed to be read in churches," that is, the churches of the established Church of England. That is about as much authority as you can get. It is also about as much reason to read "literature" as you can imagine.

This force, in the case of the King James Bible, is associated with the sovereignty of the nation-state. The authority of secular literature within Western print culture has always been distantly (or sometimes overtly) modeled on the authority of sacred scripture. The latter authority has in recent centuries tended to be sanctioned by state power. This is true even in countries, like the United States, explicitly founded on the separation of church and state. Perhaps because of this connection between state power and religion, reading the Bible in an on-line computer version that might have come from anywhere in the world does not seem, to me at least, to subject the reader to the same authority as a printed Bible does.

PLATO'S PUTDOWN OF RHAPSODIC POETRY, AND THE PUTDOWN'S PROGENY

Alfred North Whitehead said that all Western culture is a footnote to Plato, however much Plato's own work may be derivative. This is as true of Plato's ideas about poetry as of his other cardinal concepts. Plato had two theories of why to read literature. Or rather, to speak more accurately, he had two quite different reasons for why not to read literature. Both have had resonance through all the centuries since Plato. Both are still widely current, though often in disguised forms, today.

One Platonic theory of poetry is radically undercut by Socrates's irony. In the Ion, the poet, or rather the public reciter of poetry like Ion, is seen as a somewhat dangerous rhapsode. The gods or some divine afflatus speaks through the rhapsode. Using the famous figure of the magnet that charges successive rings attached in series to it, Socrates speaks of the rhapsode as the third in the chain. The true speaker in a poem with valid authority is the goddess or Muse. Both Homeric epics, the Iliad and the Odyssey, begin with invocations of the Muse. These are, in Robert Fitzgerald's translations: "Anger be now your song, immortal one . . . ," for the *Iliad*, and "Sing in me, Muse, and through me tell the story . . . ," for the *Odyssey*. Homer does not make up these epics, the invocations imply. They are sung through him. He is the ventriloquized mouthpiece of the Muse. The rhapsode, in turn, like a second magnetized ring, when he recites or chants the Homeric poems, transmits again the power mediated to him by Homer. If we read between the lines of what Socrates says, however, we can see that Socrates (and probably Plato too) is ironically sceptical of the rhapsode's claims. The *Ion* can be read as the first important demystification in our tradition of the poet's claim to speak with divine authority.

The inspired rhapsode, moreover, is, in Socrates's view (and possibly in Plato's), dangerous because he constitutes a decisive interruption in the *status quo*. The source of the rhapsode's authority is claimed to be in one way or another supernatural. It is hard to gauge the degree of irony in Socrates's seeming praise of Ion for participating in the magnetic chain that transfers Homer's inspiration to Ion as reciter of Homer. It would be a mistake, however, to take it altogether at face value:

> . . . for a poet is a light and winged thing, and holy, and never able to compose until he has become inspired, and is beside himself, and reason is no longer in him. So long as he has this [reason] in his possession, no man is able to make poetry or to chant in prophecy.

That does not quite sound like an unequivocal endorsement of the poet.

A long history of the assumption that literature is divinely inspired could be written. Such a history might begin with the Hebrew prophets and Greek poets and rhapsodes. That history would then go down through all those medieval Christian mystics who claimed direct access to visionary knowledge. They were often burned as heretics, if they were not canonized as saints. After that, came multitudinous Protestant claims to visionary authority, for example John Bunyan's. Then came secularizations of that in the Romantic doctrine of supernatural inspiration. An example is Percy Bysshe Shelley's claim in the "Defence of Poetry," in a beautiful figure James Joyce admired, that "the mind in creation is as a fading coal which some invisible influence, like an inconstant wind, awakens to transitory brightness."

For Shelley, "poets are the unacknowledged legislators of the World." They are legislators because they are the avenue through which a new power to shape society comes from divine sources, flows through the poet, and thence outward to change society. The Irish poet William Butler Yeats (1865–1939), at the end of the nineteenth century, in his *Ideas of Good and Evil*, is still affirming more or less the same doctrine as Shelley's when he says: "Solitary men in moments of contemplation receive, as I think, the creative impulse from the lowest of the Nine Hierarchies, and so make and unmake mankind, and even the world itself, for does not 'the eye altering alter all'?" The interpolated phrase, "as I think," is a characteristic Yeatsian reservation. Moreover, to say the poet's power to change the world is an alteration in perspective that makes things look different is not the same thing as to say that poets actually change the world.

Shelley's phrase, "unacknowledged legislators of the World," is more complex than it may at first appear. Poets are lawgivers. They lay down the laws by which society operates and is governed. Poets play the role of Moses or Lycurgus, those aboriginal lawgivers who established the grounding laws originating two different cultures, Hebrew and Spartan. Shelley's poets, however, are "unacknowledged legislators" (my emphasis). They operate continuously, making and remaking mankind. I take it this means that poets work surreptitiously, stealthily, invisibly, as lawgivers. People do not know what is happening to them, whereas Moses's or Lycurgus's laws were publicly announced. In Moses's case, the Ten Commandments were inscribed on the tablets of the law for everyone to read when he brought them down from Mount Sinai. Poets, Shelley seems to be implying, are legislators in the sense that they establish in those who read their work the ideological and therefore unconscious or "unacknowledged" assumptions that govern behavior in that particular society.

Modern scholars in literary criticism, in the New Historicism, or in cultural studies often make different versions of the same assumption. Anthony Trollope's novels, for example, such scholars would assert, strongly reinforce or even to some degree create the assumption that such a thing as "being in love" exists. A young woman, Trollope taught, should always guide her response to a proposal of marriage by whether or not she is "in love with" the man who has proposed to her. Trollope often overtly asserts this idea. "[I]t must ever be wrong," he says in *An Autobiography*, speaking of Lady Glencora in his *Can You Forgive Her?*, "to force a girl into a marriage with a man she does not love, – and certainly the more so when there is another whom she does love." Such assumptions are not eternally in force, everywhere, at all times, and in all cultures. Literature's authority at a particular time and place enforces them as something that comes to be seen as taken for granted and universal. Notions like "being in love" guide behavior and judgment in a particular culture at a particular moment. Trollope was an unacknowledged legislator of this ideologeme.

Just as Socrates's irony undercuts poetry's claims, so cultural critics attempt to free us from taken-for-granted assumptions by persuading us that they are no more than that – ideological assumptions, not eternal verities. To do this seems all to the good. The question then becomes, what should be put in the place of the vacancies left when we are all thoroughly free of ideology? Probably what we most often put is no more than some other set of ideological assumptions. A culture is to be defined as a social group all accepting similar assumptions about value, behavior, and judgment. A strong reason for reading literature, it might be argued, is that it is still one of the quickest ways, for better or for worse, to become acculturated, to get inside one's own culture and to belong to it. Children's literature during the print age had that as one of its main functions. That function is now more and more performed, even for small children, by television, cinema, and popular music. Reading literature is also one of the quickest ways to get inside a culture other than one's own, assuming that is possible at all and assuming you happen to want to do it.

WHY DID PLATO SO FEAR POETRY?

Plato's other concept of poetry, asserted in the _Republic_, is much more overtly negative than the one expressed in the _Ion_. It also has a long history, down to the present day. In the _Republic_, poetry is condemned and the poets exiled just because poetry is a successful "imitation." Imitation is bad for two reasons. For one thing, it is secondary, derived, not the real thing. In that sense it is factitious, however accurate it may be as a copy. A bed, for example, Plato argued, is already an

prototype

imitation of the "idea" of a bed, the ideal paradigm from which each real bed is copied. A painting of a bed or a description of it in poetry, such as Homer's description in the *Odyssey* of Odysseus's nuptial bed, with its bedpost made of a still-rooted olive tree's trunk, is at two removes. It is a copy of a copy, so who needs it?

Imitations of people in literature, moreover, in Plato's second repudiation of poetry, have a way of contaminating readers. This is his second objection to poetry in the *Republic*. Poetry is catching. Readers imagine themselves to be the heroes or heroines about whom they read. All people should remain what they are. Moral probity depends on it. Poetry leads people astray because it encourages the knack human beings have to pretend to be something or someone other than they are. Poetry makes all people actors or actresses, and everybody knows what immoral persons actors and actresses are. Plato assumes that the speakers in the *Iliad* and the *Odyssey* are Homer himself, not a fictive "narrator."As long as Homer speaks in his own voice, his speech is moral. When, however, he pretends to be Odysseus speaking and telling part of the story, immorality sets in.

One trouble with pretending to be someone or something else is that there is no stopping it. For Plato, the act of pretending rapidly runs down through a sexist chain of being from men to women to animals to inanimate objects, in a crescendo of degradation. Socrates's affirmation of this terrible danger in poetry is the classic condemnation of imitation in the Western tradition. Imitation is a species of dehumanizing or unmanning (!) madness. Poetry, for Plato, has authority all right, but it is the authority of radical evil. Therefore the poets must be banished from his ideal republic. This is the most powerful argument ever devised for why not to read literature. It should be remembered, however, that just as Plato condemns role-playing while playing the role of Socrates, so his condemnation of literature is presented within an extravagant example of literature, that is, one of the Platonic dialogues. Those dialogues, as Nietzsche asserted, arose out of the wreckage of the previous Greeks genres and contained in prototype the literary mode that is still most decisive for us today, that is, the novel.

> We will not [says Socrates] then allow our charges, whom we expect to prove good men, being men, to play the parts of women and imitate a woman young or old wrangling with her husband, defying heaven, loudly boasting, fortunate in her own conceit, or involved in misfortune and possessed by grief and lamentation – still less a woman that is sick, in love, or in labor . . . Nor may they imitate slaves, female and male, doing the offices of slaves . . . Nor yet, as it seems, bad men who are cowards and who do the opposite of the things we just now spoke of [things done by men who are "brave, sober, pious, free"], reviling and lampooning one another, speaking foul words in their cups or when sober and in other ways sinning against themselves and others in word and deed after the fashion of such men. And I take it they must not form the habit of likening themselves to madmen either in words nor yet in deeds. For while knowledge they must have both of mad and bad men and women, they must do and imitate nothing of this kind . . . Are they to imitate smiths and other craftsmen or the rowers of triremes and those who call the time to them or other things connected therewith?
>
> How could they, he [Adimantus] said, since it will be forbidden them even to pay any attention to such things?

> Well, then, neighing horses and lowing bulls, and the noise
> of rivers and the roar of the sea and the thunder and
> everything of that kind – will they imitate these?
>
> Nay, they have been forbidden, he said, to be mad or liken
> themselves to madmen.

As this eloquent passage suggests, Plato's distaste for poetry and for mimesis generally, or rather the distaste he ascribes to Socrates, is no doubt connected to his notorious distaste for the body. The body, for Plato, is, at best, a stage on the way to disembodied spirituality. Bodily love, we learn in the *Phaedrus*, must be sublimed into spiritual love. The Homeric epics, for example, are about love and war, two highly incarnated activities. Mimesis of love and war ties the soul to its earthly tomb, the body. It should therefore be forbidden in the ideal commonwealth.

THE LONG LIFE OF PLATO'S PUTDOWN OF POETRY

One aspect of James Joyce's (1882–1941) work that is deliberately defiant of his culture's traditions is his imitation through words, in *Ulysses*, of the sound, for example, a printing press makes: "Sllt. The nethermost deck of the first machine jogged forward its flyboard with sllt the first batch of quirefolded papers. Sllt. Almost human the way it sllt to call attention. Doing its level best to speak," or, at the beginning of *Finnegans Wake*, of the sound of thunder: "bababadalgharaghtakamminarronnkonnbronntonnerronntuonnthunntrovarrhounawnskawntoohoohoordenenthurnuk!" The writer, Joyce claims, can and should imitate anything in words, in an exercise of his or her sovereign authority. One shudders to think of what Plato would have thought of Molly Bloom's soliloquy at the end of *Ulysses*. The affirmation of Joycean authority takes a hyperbolic form in Stephen Daedalus's Shelleyesque vocational commitment at the end of *A Portrait of the Artist as a Young Man*: "Welcome, O life! I go to encounter for the millionth time the reality of experience and to forge in the smithy of my soul the uncreated conscience of my race."

As against such extravagant claims for the writer's authority, Plato's condemnation of the evils of imitation echoes down through the centuries in the Western tradition. An example is Protestant condemnations of novel reading. Reading novels, Protestant moralists thought, seduced young people, especially young women, to dwell in fictive worlds. That led them astray from their real-world duties.

The stern repudiation of novel reading by the great Enlightenment German philosopher Immanuel Kant (1724–1804), in his *Critique of Judgment* (1790), is a striking example of this. "Novel reading," he said, in a more or less direct echo of Plato, "weakens the memory and destroys character." Kant dislikes literature for the very reason I like it, that is, as the invitation to dwell with sympathy in a fictitious world. Kant says novel reading is bad because it is a fanaticism of sympathy for purely fictitious persons, whereas we should be deciding in the real world, with apathy not sympathy, what our ethical duties are. Novel reading is an example of what Kant, in a word he frequently used, calls *Schwärmerei*. "Fanaticism" is a feeble translation of this wonderful German word. It means also revelry, riotous behavior, enthusiasm, rapture, ecstasy over something, idolization. Fear and disdain for novel reading takes a typical sexist turn in Kant, in a passage from lecture notes made by a student:

The man is unfortunate who has a novel reader for a wife; for

> in her thoughts she has certainly already been married
> to Grandison [the hero of Samuel Richardson's *Sir
> Charles Grandison* (1753–4), wildly popular in Germany
> in the eighteenth century] and has now become a
> widow. How little desire will she then have to go into
> the kitchen!

I owe this wonderfully revealing male chauvinist passage, and the translation of it, to David Hensley. Immanuel Kant, who remained unmarried, spent little time reading novels, it seems clear, during those cold and dark winter evenings in Königsberg. Or if he read them, he did so furtively and guiltily.

Novels themselves, in certain notorious cases, represent their own moral badness. This is an oblique self-affirmation of their dangerous authority. A novel sometimes presents within itself an indirect warning to the reader to put down the book he or she is at that moment reading. Catherine Morland, the heroine of Jane Austen's (1775–1817) *Northanger Abbey*, Flaubert's (1821–80) Emma Bovary, Conrad's (1857–1924) Lord Jim, and many other fictional characters were morally corrupted and led to have absurd expectations about themselves and about the world by reading novels. Cervantes's (1547–1616) Don Quixote is of course the archetype for this motif. Henry James follows this tradition when he has the gifted actress, Miriam Rooth, heroine of *The Tragic Muse*, lack a fixed character of her own, just because she is so good an actress. She is nothing but whatever role she happens to be playing, even in "real life." Peter Sherringham, the rising young diplomat who falls in love with Miriam, has played Pygmalion to her as Galatea. He pays for her training as an actress. Sherringham reflects at one crucial moment in the novel on Miriam's strange and distressing lack of character. You never know where to have her:

> It came over him suddenly that so far from there being any question of her having the histrionic nature she simply had it in such perfection that she was always acting; that her existence was a series of parts assumed for the moment, each changed for the next, before the perpetual mirror of some curiosity or admiration or wonder – some spectatorship that she perceived or imagined in the people about her . . . [Her] identity resided in the continuity of her personations, so that she had no moral privacy, as he phrased it to himself, but lived in a high wind of exhibition, of figuration – such a woman was a kind of monster in whom of necessity there would be nothing to "be fond" of, because there would be nothing to take hold of . . . The girl's face made it vivid to him now – the discovery that she positively had no countenance of her own, but only the countenance of the occasion, a sequence, a variety – capable possibly of becoming immense – of representative movements.

A plausible case could be made for seeing my childhood submission to *The Swiss Family Robinson* as pernicious escapism. It was the beginning of a bad habit that has kept me in life-long subservience to fantasies and fictions rather than soberly engaged in "the real world" and in fulfilling my responsibilities there. I can, to tell the truth, still remember my mother's voice when she exhorted me to stop reading and go outside to play. Proust's Marcel, an inveterate reader as a child, received similar admonitions, as perhaps Proust himself did. Children nowadays who spend all the time they can watching television or playing computer games are not all that different from the habitual reader in the now fading heyday of print culture. A computer game is another kind of virtual reality, as is a network news program, not to speak of a television drama. These are no doubt less valuable fictive worlds, we inveterate readers of "canonical" texts would assert. The difference, however, is perhaps not so great as we might wish.

Jeremy Bentham (1748–1832), an English philosopher with a utilitarian cast of mind, said that poetry has about as much use value as a game of pushpin (whatever that is). He meant this as a supreme putdown. In comparing literature to computer games, I am not saying the same thing as what Bentham said. I am saying that both a literary work and a computer game create an imaginary reality for those who read the work or play the game. I am also saying that both computer games and literature have irreplaceable social utility, though of a different sort in each case. After all, are not both *Alice's Adventures in Wonderland* and *Through the Looking-Glass* modeled, in different ways, on games, the first on a game of cards, the second on a chess game. For Carroll, at least, and for me too, a deep congruence exists between storytelling and games.

ARISTOTLE'S DEFENSE OF POETRY

Aristotle's *Poetics*, the greatest ancient treatise on poetry, was lectures on what we today call literature, or rather on those quite special forms of it, Greek epic and tragedy. Those forms had a social function quite different from that performed by literature during the print epoch. Aristotle's lectures were partly in response to Plato's double condemnation of poetry. Tragedy and epic were for Aristotle the paradigmatic forms of "poetry." He saw these as embedded in the social reality they served. They had a pragmatic, down-to-earth function within it. As against Plato, Aristotle unashamedly praises imitations, for two good social reasons. We learn from imitating, says Aristotle, and we take pleasure in imitations. "As to the origin of the poetic art as a whole," asserts Aristotle in his imperturbably reasonable (and sexist) way,

> it stands to reason that two operative causes brought it into being, both of them rooted in human nature. Namely (1) the habit of imitating is congenital to human beings from childhood (actually man [!] differs from the other animals in that he is the most imitative and learns his first lessons through imitation), and so is (2) the pleasure that all men take in works of imitation.

A tragedy, says Aristotle, is an imitation of an action. That action, most often, is embodied in a story or myth that all the spectators of the tragedy already know, for example Oedipus's story. Those stories generally have to do with the enigmatic and inscrutable relations between gods and men or women. An example is the unanswered question, in Sophocles's *Oedipus the King*, of why the god Apollo has decided to punish Oedipus so cruelly by making him unintentionally kill his father and marry his mother. Even so, the social function of tragedy, for Aristotle, is this-worldly and even bodily. It purges from body and soul the bad emotions of pity and fear by arousing them. Aristotle sees tragedy, in Gerard Else's translation, as an imitation of an action that "through a course of pity and fear complet[es] the purification [*Katharsis*] of tragic acts which have those emotional characteristics," or, in S. H. Butcher's translation, "through pity and fear effecting the proper purgation of those emotions." A tragedy functions thereby as a species of cathartic homeopathy.

That is, however, just one way to read the somewhat

enigmatic lecture notes that make up Aristotle's *Poetics*. These have puzzled commentators down through the centuries. It is also possible to read Aristotle as saying the arousing of pity and fear by a tragedy is a good in itself, a reason to attend the play, even if these emotions are not purged. Why? Because these emotions are in themselves pleasurable and pleasure is good. In one place in the *Poetics*, Aristotle says that

> the plot must be so structured, even without benefit of any visual effect, that the one who is hearing the events shudders with fear and feels pity at what happens: which is what one would experience on hearing the plot of the *Oedipus* . . . Since it is the pleasure derived from pity and fear by means of imitation that the poet should seek to produce, it is clear that these qualities must be built into the constituent events.

Here nothing is said about "catharsis." Only the pleasure of the unpurged emotions is stressed. The word "kartharsis" appears only once in the *Poetics*. That imitations give pleasure is one of Aristotle's defenses of poetry. The catharsis or purification, in Gerard Else's translation, is not of the bad emotions of pity and fear, but of "tragic acts which have those emotional characteristics." This would link tragedy to its sources in rituals of purification that were repeated in outward dramatized events displaying purifications, for example the curing of the plague in Thebes by eliminating Oedipus, its cause.

As Paul Gordon has shown in *Tragedy After Nietzsche: Rapturous Superabundance*, Aristotle is anxious to expel the irrational in his account of tragedy. At the same time, he is almost obsessively concerned with different forms of the irrational. Aristotle's makes a claim to a rational mastery of the irrational that is like Oedipus's. In doing so he repeats the pattern of his paradigmatic tragedy, *Oedipus the King*, with its roots in Dionysiac rituals. Aristotle recognized, more or less in spite of himself, that tragedy is drawn toward that Dionysiac center it would expel. Aristotle's admission that the pity and fear generated by a tragedy is pleasurable and that such pleasure is a good is not far from Nietzsche's praise of Dionysiac irrational excess as essential not just to tragedy but to art in general.

In either reading (and there are others) of the *Poetics*, the authority of a tragedy, for Aristotle, does not derive from its author, but from its embeddedness in society. Literature is a complex institution using myths known and owned by everyone for a specific collective social purpose.

ARISTOTLE LIVES!

surrounding

Aristotle's assumptions about why we should read literature or witness the performance of plays still have force in different permutations. An example is the widespread nineteenth- and twentieth-century assumption that literature is placed within its general circumambient culture as a public institution. Literature draws its authority from its social function. Its validity is conferred on it by its users and by those journalists and critics that ascribe value to it. The literary work's authority derives sometimes from the belief that the work is an accurate representation of social reality and its reigning ideological assumptions. Sometimes the conferred authority derives from a belief that literature shapes social structures and beliefs. It does this through effective deployment of what Kenneth Burke calls "a strategy for encompassing a situation." The latter hypothesis recognizes a strong performative function for literature. In both these forms, however, literature's authority is social. That authority is conferred from outside literature, often by belief in its truth of correspondence to social things as they are. This conviction is present in Aristotle's famous claim that poetry is "a more philosophical and serious business than history." This is so because literature presents not what actually happened but what "can happen." Poetry, says Aristotle, is "universal." It presents "what kind of person is likely to do or say certain kinds of things, according to probability or necessity."

Charles Dickens (1812–70) reaffirms the assumption that good literature is validated by its truth of correspondence when he defends *Oliver Twist*, in the preface to the third edition (1841), by claiming that the representation of Nancy is "TRUE." Later in his career Dickens defends, also in a preface, the spontaneous combustion of Krook in *Bleak House* in the same way. Dickens adduces a whole series of supposed historical cases of spontaneous combustion – in Verona, in Reims, in Columbus, Ohio. Recent evidence, quite suprisingly to me, has confirmed Dickens's belief, though such cases are not truly "spontaneous." They need some external source of combustion, a fire in a fireplace for example that ignites the victim, though he or she combusts in the same horribly slow way that Dickens describes as Krook's fate. The body fat burns like candle wax. The victim's clothes serve as the wick. Does that modern scientific corroboration give Krook's spontaneous combustion in *Bleak House* greater authority in a present-day reader's eyes? It would be hard to deny that it does.

In this tradition, to sum up, we should read literature because it gives socially useful pleasure and because it is seen to have representatational validity. These assumptions have had tremendous force in nineteenth- and twentieth-century Europe and America. They are basic presuppositions of most pedagogy and critical writing even today.

LITERATURE AS DISGUISED AUTOBIOGRAPHY

Some supernatural grounding authority, the solid reality of the extra-verbal social world as ground, the sheer bad or good power of "fictions" to generate behavior-changing credence in those who submit themselves to them – all these sources of literature's authority have had force throughout the Western tradition. They have had force, often, in the same societies or in the same writers and readers at once, in living contradictions that are often not even noticed. The role of literature in nineteenth- and twentieth-century European and American cultures has been no more than a special case of this incoherent mix.

A fourth ground of literature's authority will complete my repertoire of the stories we have told ourselves to explain why we should read (or not read) literature. Not only are these stories incoherent among themselves. They are also unable to contain, to explain, or to reduce to order the immense abundance of incommensurable universes that make up that part of the universal library to which we give the name "literature." The invention of something called "the Western tradition" is itself part of literature. It is one of the most beguiling and enchanting of fictive universes. Another way to put this is to say that the concept of "the Western tradition" is ideological, rather than being, as Dickens said of Nancy, "TRUE."

 Roland Barthes had to exert some effort to kill off the author, in "The Death of the Author (La mort de l'auteur [1968])," because it is so strong a part of our tradition to believe that what gives the literary work its authority is the author who stands behind it. The author validates the work, gives it a solid ground. An immense amount of recent research, especially on English and continental Renaissance literature, has persuaded many people that selfhood is "constructed." Selfhood is a matter of "self-fashioning." It is not innate, inborn, or God-given. Selfhood, according to such a view, is a product of surrounding ideological and cultural forces, including of course those embodied in what we would now call "literary works." Montaigne's essays, for example, are, among other things, a reflection on the variability and diversity from time to time of the self. The self, the "moi," is "ondoyant et divers," wavering and diverse. A good many people from Shakespeare's day to the present have nevertheless gone on believing that selfhood is God-given, fixed, unitary, and permanent from birth. Confidence in that is an important a part of our religious and legal traditions, whether Christian, Judaic, or Muslim. How could the law hold someone morally or legally responsible for an act if he or she is not the same person from moment to moment? To believe the self is wavering and diverse provides a marvelous cop out from moral responsibility. It allows you to say, "That was a different me who promised to do that. You can't blame me for not doing it."

In both cases, however, whether selfhood is seen as constructed or as innate, the notion that the author is the authorizing source and guarantee of a work has in different ways had wide allegiance in the West. This might be defined by saying that the author tends to be held responsible for what he or she has written. He or she is held responsible, for example, by censoring authorities, by the reading public, or by scholars and teachers. The latter support that stance by writing or giving courses on "Shakespeare," or "Dickens," or "Emily Dickinson," meaning the works that they are presumed on good authority to have written. An enormous industry of biographical scholarship and popular writing, from Samuel Johnson's *Lives of the Poets* down to the latest "authoritative biography" of some canonical or non-canonical writer, reinforces the assumption that you can blame the author for what he or she has written. It follows that you can understand the work by knowing about its author.

Popular media outlets like the *The New York Times Book Review* or *The New York Review of Books* tend today to review all biographies, good or bad, of famous or not so famous authors, while ignoring much serious critical works on those same authors. The genre of the interview is another example of this interest in the author. The interview is a feature of the media worldwide. I myself, to give a peripheral example, have been interviewed repeatedly in the Peoples Republic of China and elsewhere. I imagine far more people in China have read interviews of me in newspapers and magazines than have read my work, even though some of that has been translated into Chinese. Jacques Derrida has been interviewed so often and is so eloquent in response even to banal questions that he has published a distinguished book made exclusively of interviews, *Points de Suspension* (1992), translated as *Points* ... (1995).

"An explorer of human terrain," by Mel Gussow, an interview of the United States African-American author Alice Walker, in "The Arts" section of *The New York Times*, for December 26, 2000, represents all the complex intertwined ideology that lies behind the interview as a genre. To call Walker "an explorer of human terrain" presumes that the human terrain is there to be explored. The writer is like a scientist or ethnographer writing a description of what he or she has found in a voyage of exploration. Gussow's story is accompanied by a charming photograph of Alice Walker herself in her Berkeley, California, house. She has a big smile and looks like a nice person. The assumption of this interview is that readers will be more interested in the author than in his or her writings. The reader will see the latter as flowing directly from the psychology of the former. Though the ostensible occasion of Gussow's interview is the recent publication of a new book of stories by Walker, *The Way Forward is With a Broken Heart*, practically nothing is said about the stories except about their directly autobiographical content. According to Gussow, the stories represent or reflect Walker's love for Melvyn Leventhal, a white civil rights lawyer, and the eventual breakup of her marriage to him. The authority of Walker's stories is their more or less direct expression of her life. This means that their accuracy in representing "the real world," as she has experienced it, is the guarantee of their worth. Implicit in Gussow's concentration on Walker's life in his interview is the idea that if you know all about that life you will hardly need to read her work.

Along with that assumption, an idea of inspiration that at least distantly echoes Plato's *Ion* surfaces, momentarily and incongruously, in Gussow's interview. Perhaps its appearance can be justified as just something Walker happens to believe. Walker, the reader is told, thinks of her work as giving a life beyond the grave to the previous generations of her family:

"It was heartbreaking to think that somehow they wouldn't survive in a form that was faithful to them – who they were and the way they sounded," she said. Through her writing she has been able to lend a certain fulfillment to lives that had been limited.

The granting of survival through words in Walker's most famous work, *The Color Purple*, occurred through an act of creation in which Walker was "beside herself" and wrote almost like a spirit medium through whom her characters spoke:

> After her divorce she wrote *The Color Purple*, and it was a bolt of inspiration. She wrote it so fast, in longhand in a little spiral notebook, that it was "almost like dictation." As an artist, she says, she is a conduit for her mother and their relatives . . . In a postscript to *The Color Purple*, she called herself an "author and medium."

The ideological complex assumed in "An explorer of human terrain" is so ubiquitous in our culture, that an author is unlikely to avoid being held responsible for what he or she has written by saying, "Don't blame me. I am just an insubstantial and baseless construction of the ideology of my gender, class, and race. I cannot help writing the way I do." Nor can an author escape responsibility by saying something like the following, as Jacques Derrida says he or she can do within a democracy that recognizes a right to free speech,

> Don't blame me. That is not me speaking, but an imagined, created, fictive narrator. I am exercising my right to say anything, to put anything in question. Don't make the naïve mistake of confusing the narrative voice with the author. I am not an axe-murderer. I am just imagining what it would be like to be one in my *Crime and Punishment*.

The almost unanimous response to this would be to say,

> That excuse won't wash. You wrote it, and by way of whatever cunningly devised relays and cover-ups, those words came from your subjectivity and are authorized by you as writing subject. We hold you responsible for what you have written and for all its effects, good and bad.

If the author has been granted enormous authority in our culture as the authorizing source of what he or she has published, this authority has taken two distinct forms. The author has had attributed to him or her a constative power, the power to tell the truth, to represent accurately his or her circumambient society. The author has sometimes also been assumed to have what might be called a performative authority. This would be the power to manipulate words in such a way that they will operate as speech acts.

What Anthony Trollope says in *An Autobiography* about the novelist's responsibility to tell the truth may be taken as an example of the first form of authorial authority. Trollope firmly believes that it is the duty of novelists to teach virtue in their novels. He believes that the chief means of doing this is to tell the truth, the whole truth, and nothing but the truth about human life:

> By either [poetry or novels], false sentiment may be fostered, false notions of humanity may be engendered, false honour, false love, false worship may be created; by either, vice instead of virtue may be taught. But by each, equally, may true honour, true love, true worship, and true humanity be inculcated; and that will be the greatest teacher who will spread such truth the widest.

The reader will note that Trollope here mixes constative and performative language. The novelist's primary responsibility is a constative one: to tell the truth, but this truth-telling is performatively effective. It "engenders," "creates," or "inculcates" either virtue or vice in the novelist's readers.

Just how this magic charm may work to make a literary text a felicitous speech act, Henry James's preface to Volume 15 of his collected novels and tales (the "New York Edition") makes explicit. The volume contains a set of short stories about writers, including "The Lesson of the Master," "The Death of the Lion," "The Figure in the Carpet." Several of these were first published in Henry Harland's somewhat notorious *fin de siècle* journal, *The Yellow Book*. Responding to the charge made by a friend that the writer-protagonists of those stories are "unrealistic" because no writer with a selfless dedication to high art, no "artist enamoured of perfection, ridden by his idea or paying for his sincerity," exists these days in England, James retorts:

> If the life about us for the last thirty years refuses warrant for these examples, then so much the worse for that life. The *constatation* would be so deplorable that instead of making it we must dodge it: there are decencies that in the name of the general self-respect we must take for granted, there's a kind of rudimentary intellectual honour to which we must, in the interest of civilisation, at least pretend.

There are, it seems, times when it is "indecent" to tell the truth in an accurate constatation.

If such representations as Neil Paraday, Henry St. George, and Hugh Vereker (heroes of three stories in this volume) do not have the authority of being accurate copies of social and historical truth, where then do they get their validity? James gives two answers. One is to confess that these characters are drawn from the depths of his own mind and intimate experience:

> . . . the material for any picture of personal states so specifically complicated as those of my hapless friends in the present volume will have been drawn preponderantly from

the depths of the designer's own mind . . . [T]he states
represented, the embarrassments and predicaments studied,
the tragedies and comedies recorded, can be intelligibly
fathered but on his own intimate experience.

The confession that these stories are autobiographical is all
well and good, but how does a "designer" generate belief in
such fictions in his or her readers and so give those fictions at
least a spurious authority? The answer is that the writer cun-
ningly and deliberately manipulates words so as to make
them performatively efficacious charms. As such, they induce
trust and belief in the reader. This might be paralleled by
Albertine's "charming art of lying with simplicity (l'art
charmant qu'elle avait de mentir avec simplicité)," that
beguiles Marcel, in Proust's *À la recherche du temps perdu*. Marcel is
led by Albertine's artful lying, for example, into believing that
Bergotte was still alive and able to carry on a conversation
with Albertine when he was already dead. In another case, her
lies, he says, would lead him to believe that he had seen
Albertine having a conversation in the street with a woman
whom he knew for certain had been absent from Paris for
months. Suppose, says Marcel, I had happened to be in
the street at that time and had seen with my own eyes that
Albertine had not encountered the woman:

I should then have known that Albertine was lying. But is this
absolutely certain even then? . . . A strange darkness (Une
obscurité sacrée) would have clouded my mind, I should have
begun to doubt whether I had seen her alone, I should hardly
even have sought to understand by what optical illusion I had
failed to perceive the lady, and I should not have been greatly
surprised to find myself mistaken (trompé), for the stellar
universe is not so difficult of comprehension as the real

actions of other people, especially of the people we love, fortified as they are against our doubts by fables devised for their protection (fortifiés qu'ils sont contre notre doute par des fables destinées à les protéger).

Here is Henry James's description of a similar conjuring force on the writer's part. In James's case it is a dangerous performative power in an author to engender trust in the reader in what is not really true to life:

And then, I'm not ashamed to allow, it was *amusing* to make these people "great," so far as one could do so without making them intrinsically false . . . It was amusing because it was more difficult – from the moment, of course I mean, that one worked out at all their greatness; from the moment one didn't simply give it to be taken on trust. Working out economically almost anything is the very life of the art of representation; just as the request to take on trust, tinged with the least extravagance, is the very death of the same. (There may be such a state of mind brought about on the reader's part, I think, as a positive desire to take on trust; but that is only the final fruit of insidious proceedings, operative to a sublime end, on the author's side; and it is at any rate a different matter.)

The writer is a species of confidence man, this passage seems to say. The last thing a confidence man should do is to make a direct appeal to be taken on trust. That would give the game away. The writer as confidence man must take a different tack. By various "insidious proceedings" of word manipulation the author must put together a text that will induce the reader to take on trust a fiction that has no provable correspondence to reality. James is describing here, strictly speaking, a form of speech act or of what speech act theorists call performative language, a way of doing something with words. In this case, it is the speech act basic to literature: using words as a conjuring power that charms the reader into believing in a fiction or at least into suspending disbelief. Commenting on the "all-ingenious 'Figure in the Carpet,'" James says, "Here exactly is a good example for you of the virtue of your taking on trust – when I have artfully begotten in you a disposition."

LITERATURE AS SPEECH ACT

My exploration of the various ways authority has been claimed for literature has culminated, with James's help, in a recognition that this authority derives from a performative use of language artfully begetting in the reader a disposition to take on trust. This is a disposition to accept at face value the virtual reality the reader enters when he or she reads a given work. That certainly happens, for example to me when I read *The Swiss Family Robinson* as a child or even when I read it again now. The problem with this view of literature is that, somewhat paradoxically, given what James says, it cuts the literary work off from its author. If Jacques Derrida, Paul de Man, and I are right, the performative and cognitive functions of language are incompatible. As de Man puts this, speaking of "the disjunction of the performative from the cognitive":

> any speech act produces an excess of cognition, but it can never hope to know the process of its own production (the only thing worth knowing) . . . Performative rhetoric and cognitive rhetoric, the rhetoric of tropes, fail to converge.

Reading James's "The Death of the Lion" or "The Figure in the Carpet" gives knowledge of the virtual reality the story generates, but the reader can never know whether this is just what James intended. The work has such an effect as it does happen to have on a given reader. This occurs within the limits of its words' performative power. If each work is, as I claim, singular, its performative effect will be singular, not fully authorized by prior conventions. It will be a form of speech act not condoned in standard speech act theory. The performative effect of the work is, moreover, dissociated from authorial intent or knowledge. This disjunction is already anticipated by the father of speech act theory, J. L. Austin when he tries, at least momentarily, to separate the "felicity" of a speech act from the subjective intention of the one who enunciates it. If I can always say, "I did not mean what I said," and thereby get out of a promise or a commitment, then the way is open for bigamists, welshers on bets, and other such low people to get away with it. It is better, Austin affirms, to say, "My word is my bond." It does not matter what I was thinking when I uttered such and such words or wrote them. The effect they have must be honored. That Austin a few pages later welshes on this commitment and makes sincerity a condition of a felicitous performative is a major crux or contradiction in his speech act theory. He has to have it both ways, but of course he cannot logically have it both ways. What is relevant to my argument here is Austin's first claim, that the words must be seen to work on their own, whatever their utterer intends.

If this assumption is applied to literature considered as a speech act, particularly if we think, as I believe we should, of each work as unique, singular, *sui generis*, then this returns me to where I was at the beginning, when I was enchanted by *The Swiss Family Robinson*. *The Swiss Family Robinson* acted on me in the way it did without my having any knowledge whatsoever about the author or about what he thought he was doing in the novel. The work worked. It worked to open up a meta-reality reachable in no other way and impossible to account for fully by its author's designs or by any other feature of the reading act's context. The literary work is self-authorizing.

Insofar as a literary work is seen as performative rather than constative, it must be subject to the general law of non-cognizability that governs speech acts. Something will happen when a work is read, but just what will happen cannot be fully foreseen, foreknown, or controlled. Every teacher of literature knows, often to his or her dismay, what strange and unpredictable things happen when students read an assigned work. Each literary work creates or reveals a world, a world furnished with characters possessed of imaginary bodies, speeches, feelings, and thoughts. These characters dwell surrounded by buildings, streets, a landscape, weather, and so on, in short, in a alternative reality complete with inhabitants rather like ourselves. It seems as if that reality has been waiting somewhere to be uncovered, exposed, transmitted or "beamed" to the reader by the words on the page. This is analogous to the way more modern technologies create virtual realities on the screen or in the perception of the one who wears a virtual reality apparatus. The book we hold in our hands when we read The Swiss Family Robinson or J. M. Coetzee's Foe is a virtual reality apparatus.

Whether or not the virtual reality we enter when we read a novel by Trollope or by James, or a poem by Yeats, pre-existed and is revealed by the author in an act of response to it or whether it is factitiously created by the words the author has chosen or has happened to write, cannot be decided. No evidence exists to adjudicate certainly between these two alternatives. The authority of literature remains poised

between these two possibilities. It is impossible to decide
between them, though nothing could be more important,
both for a definition of literature and for an explanation of
why to read literary works, than to know decisively, once and
for all.

Five

TEACHING HOW TO READ IS A MUG'S GAME

Telling someone who knows how to read how to read is a mug's game, as T. S. Eliot said of poetry writing. He presumably meant poetry writing requires a lot of swotting up. According to the *Oxford English Dictionary*, "mug" is, or was, a slang term at Oxford for a student who studies a lot, a "grind." "To mug" is "to get up (a subject) by hard study." Eliot may also have meant that a poet is like a "mug" in the sense of being criminal, another (United States) meaning of the word. He notoriously said meaning in a poem is like the piece of meat the burglar gives to the watchdog so he can get inside the house. Teaching reading is a mug's game in both senses. You have to know a lot, all about tropes, for example, not to speak of history and literary history. Moreover, as these last two chapters will suggest, what you are teaching is by no means an innocent skill.

Teaching reading also seems unnecessary. If you can read, you can read. Who needs any more help? Just how someone gets from illiteracy to literacy or from basic literacy to being a "good reader" remains something of a mystery. A talent for irony, for example, is a requisite for good reading. Sensitivity to irony seems to be unevenly distributed in the population. A sense for irony is by no means identical to intelligence. You get it or you don't get it. Dickens in *Bleak House* in what he says about Jo the crossing sweeper has movingly imagined, for us readers, what it must be like not to be able to read:

> It must be a strange state to be like Jo! To shuffle through the streets, unfamiliar with the shapes and in utter darkness as to the meaning, of those mysterious symbols, so abundant over the shops, and the corner of streets, and on the doors, and in the windows! To see people read, and to see people write, and to see the postman deliver letters, and not to have the least idea of all that language – to be, to every scrap of it, stone blind and dumb!

A blindness to irony, even in someone who can "read" perfectly well, is not altogether unlike Jo's blank incomprehension.

Probably what actually happens within a given person's mind and feelings when he or she has "learned to read," and reads a given page, differs more than one might wish, or expect, from person to person. Teachers, those incurable optimists in a discouraging situation, often want to assume that the same thing happens to all their students when they follow directions to "Read *Bleak House* by next Tuesday," or "Read the following poems by Yeats for Friday's class." In my experience, dismayingly diverse things happen when students do that. Or, alternatively, one might rejoice at the way students resist being poured into a mold. Getting hard data about what actually happens when students read an "assignment" is not all that easy. It is as hard to ascertain this as it is to learn other important things about the interiority of another person, for example just what he or she means when saying "I love you," or just how colors look to another person.

Still instructive are the wild divergences and "misreadings"

I. A. Richards found, and reported in *Practical Criticism*, when he asked students to respond to poems he circulated as "hand outs." These students were relatively homogeneous Cambridge undergraduates. They had more or less the same class backgrounds and the same earlier educations. Nevertheless, they not only "got the poems wrong," by most educated people's standards, misunderstanding them, as well as judging the good ones bad and the bad ones good. They also got the poems wrong in diverse and not easily classifiable ways.

Almost universal literacy has been a major component of print culture and the concomitant rise of the democratic nation-state. As Patricia Crain has shown in *The Story of A*, teaching the alphabet to children through "alphabet books" was, within print culture, a major way of indoctrinating them into the reigning ideologies of an increasingly capitalist and consumerist culture. "A is for Apple Pie," for example, invites the child to think of learning the alphabet as connected to eating, and what could be more American than apple pie? After the child learns to read, children's books, for example *The Swiss Family Robinson*, then continue the work of making children model citizens. Nowadays, literacy is perhaps less and less necessary for that work. Television and cinema do the same job of interpellation by way of visual and aural images. The children's television show *Sesame Street* teaches the alphabet and phonics. Its real teaching power, however, is in the skits and puppet shows that powerfully indoctrinate even those who cannot read. That is not necessarily a bad thing. It seems a feature of language possession that human beings should join together in "communities" of people who see and judge things in similar ways, though no conceivable society is without its prejudices and injustices. That is one reason why democracy is always "to come." It is a far-off horizon of justice toward which all should work.

Well, then, assuming one still wants to read literature, how should one do it? I make two contradictory and not easily reconcilable prescriptions. I call these, taken together, the aporia of reading.

READING AS SCHWÄRMEREI

If it is really the case, as I have argued, that each literary work opens up a singular world, attainable in no other way than by reading that work, then reading should be a matter of giving one's whole mind, heart, feelings, and imagination, without reservation, to recreating that world within oneself, on the basis of the words. This would be a species of that fanaticism, or rapture, or even revelry that Immanuel Kant calls "Schwärmerei." The work comes alive as a kind of internal theater that seems in a strange way independent of the words on the page. That was what happened to me when I first read *The Swiss Family Robinson*. The ability to do that is probably more or less universal, once you have learned to read, once you have learned, that is, to turn those mute and objectively meaningless shapes into letters, words, and sentences that correspond to spoken language.

I suspect that my interior theater or revelry is not by any means the same as another person's. Even so, each reader's imaginary world, generated by a given work, seems to that reader to have unquestionable authority. One empirical test of this is the reaction many people have when they see a film made from a novel they have read: "No, No! It's not at all like that! They've got it all wrong."

The illustrations, particularly of children's books, play an important role in shaping that imaginary theater. The original Sir John Tenniel (1820–1914) illustrations for the Alice books told me how to imagine Alice, the White Rabbit, Tweedledum and Tweedledee, and the rest. Still, my imaginary world behind the looking-glass exceeded even the Tenniel pictures. Henry James, in *A Small Boy and Others*, paid homage to the power of George Cruikshank's (1792–1878) illustrations for *Oliver Twist* to determine the way that imaginary world seemed to him:

> It perhaps even seemed to me more Cruikshank's than Dickens's; it was a thing of such vividly terrible images, and all marked with that peculiarity of Cruikshank that the offered flowers or goodnesses, the scenes and figures intended to comfort and cheer, present themselves under his hand as but more subtly sinister, or more suggestively queer, than the frank badnesses and horrors.

What reader, who has happened to see them, to give two other examples, has not had his or her imagination shaped by the wonderful photographs by Coburn that are used as frontispieces for the New York Edition of James's works or by the frontispiece photographs for the Wessex or Anniversary Editions of Thomas Hardy's work?

I am advocating, as the first side of the aporia of reading, an innocent, childlike abandonment to the act of reading, without suspicion, reservation, or interrogation. Such a reading makes a willing suspension of disbelief, in Coleridge's famous phrase. It is a suspension, however, that does not even know anymore that disbelief might be possible. The suspension then becomes no longer the result of a conscious effort of will. It becomes spontaneous, without forethought. My analogy with reciprocal assertions of "I love you" by two persons is more than casual. As Michel Deguy says, "La poésie comme l'amour risque tout sur des signes. (Poetry, like love, risks everything on signs.)" The relation between reader and story read is like a love affair. In both cases, it is a matter of giving yourself without reservation to the other. A book in my hands or on the shelf utters a powerful command: "Read me!" To do so is as risky, precarious, or even dangerous as to respond to another person's "I love you" with an "I love you too." You never know where saying that might lead you, just as you never know where reading a given book might lead you. In my own case, reading certain books has been decisive for my life. Each such book has been a turning point, the marker of a new epoch.

Reading, like being in love, is by no means a passive act. It takes much mental, emotional, and even physical energy. Reading requires a positive effort. One must give all one's faculties to re-creating the work's imaginary world as fully and as vividly as possible within oneself. For those who are no longer children, or childlike, a different kind of effort is necessary too. This is the attempt, an attempt that may well not succeed, to suspend ingrained habits of "critical" or suspicious reading.

If this double effort, a positive one and a negative one, is not successful, it is not even possible to know what might be dangerous about submission to the magic power of the words on the page. In a similar way, you can hardly hear a piece of music as music if all your attention is taken up in identifying technical details of the score or in thinking about echoes of earlier music. You must become as a little child if you are to read literature rightly.

A certain speed in reading is necessary to accomplish this actualization, just as is the case with music. If you linger too long over the words, they lose their power as windows on the hitherto unknown. If you play a Mozart piano sonata or one of Bach's *Goldberg Variations* too slowly it does not sound like music. A proper tempo is required. The same thing is true for reading considered as the generation of a virtual reality. One must read rapidly, *allegro*, in a dance of the eyes across the page.

Not all readers are able to read all literary works in this way. I much prefer Emily Brontë's (1818–48) *Wuthering Heights* to Charlotte Brontë's (1816–55) *Jane Eyre*. I feel I ought to admire the latter more than I do, since so many good readers like it. *Jane Eyre* seems to me a sentimental wish-fulfillment, in its grand climax of Jane's marriage to a blinded and maimed Rochester, symbolically castrated: "Reader, I married him." I have the same resistance to D. H. Lawrence (1885–1930). The climactic scene in *Women in Love*, in which Ursula and Birkin finally make love, seems to me laughable, not in itself, but in Lawrence's overblown language for it: "She had her desire fulfilled. He had his desire fulfilled. For she was to him what he was to her, the immemorial magnificence of mystic, palpable, real otherness." Wow! This seems to me simply silly. Seeing something as silly deprives it of the power to open a new world. It becomes dead letters on the page. Other readers will have other candidates. I find Anthony Trollope's novels consistently enchanting, both in their recreation of Victorian middle-class ideology and in their implicit critique of that ideology. I know someone who finds Trollope's work annoying in what she sees as its false presentation of female psychology.

GOOD READING IS SLOW READING

Good reading, however, also demands slow reading, not just the dancing *allegro*. A good reader is someone on whom nothing in a text is lost, as James said a good writer is in relation to life: "Try to be one of those on whom nothing is lost." That means just the opposite of a willing suspension of disbelief that no longer even remembers the disbelief that was willingly suspended. It means the reading *lento* that Friedrich Nietzsche advocates. Such a reader pauses over every key word or phrase, looking circumspectly before and after, walking rather than dancing, anxious not to let the text put anything over on him or her. "When I picture to myself a perfect reader," says Nietzsche, "I always picture a monster of courage and curiosity, also something supple, cunning, cautious, a born adventurer and discoverer." Slow reading, critical reading, means being suspicious at every turn, interrogating every detail of the work, trying to figure out by just what means the magic is wrought. This means attending not to the new world that is opened up by the work, but to the means by which that opening is brought about. The difference between the two ways of reading might be compared to the difference between being taken in by the dazzling show of the wizard in *The Wizard of Oz* and, on the contrary, seeing the shabby showman behind the facade, pulling levers and operating the machinery, creating a factitious illusion.

This demystification has taken two forms throughout our tangled tradition. These two forms are still dominant today. One is what might be called "rhetorical reading." Such reading means a close attention to the linguistic devices by which the magic is wrought: observations of how figurative language is used, of shifts in point of view, of that all-important irony. Irony is present, for example, in discrepancies between what the narrator in a novel knows and what the narrator solemnly reports the characters as knowing, thinking, and feeling. A rhetorical reader is adept in all the habits of "close reading."

The other form of critical reading is interrogation of the way a literary work inculcates beliefs about class, race, or gender relations. These are seen as modes of vision, judgment, and action presented as objectively true but actually ideological. They are linguistic fictions masking as referential verities. This mode of demystification goes these days by the name of "cultural studies" or, sometimes, of "postcolonial studies."

Literary works, it should be remembered, have always had a powerful critical function. They challenge hegemonic ideologies, as well as reinforcing them. Literature in the modern Western sense, as a concomitant of print culture, has taken full advantage of the right to free speech. Proust's depiction of Marcel's infatuation with Albertine in *À la recherche du temps perdu* presents his mystification so powerfully that the reader shares in it. The reader finds the imaginary Albertine irresistibly attractive, charming liar though she is. Proust also remorsely deconstructs that infatuation. He shows it to be based on misreadings, illusions. Cultural criticism continues and makes more obvious a critical penchant of literature itself within Western print culture. Nevertheless, both these forms of critique – rhetorical reading and cultural criticism – have as one of their effects depriving literary works, for given readers, of the sovereign power they have when they are read *allegro*.

paradox

THE APORIA OF READING

The two ways of reading I am advocating, the innocent way and the demystified way, go counter to one another. Each prevents the other from working – hence the aporia of reading. Combining these two modes of reading in one act of reading is difficult, perhaps impossible, since each inhibits and forbids the other. How can you give yourself wholeheartedly to a literary work, let the work do its work, and at the same time distance yourself from it, regard it with suspicion, and take it apart to see what makes it tick? How can one read *allegro* and at the same time *lento*, combining the two tempos in an impossible dance of reading that is fast and slow at once?

Why, in any case, would anyone want to deprive literature of its amazing power to open alternative worlds, innumerable virtual realities? It seems like a nasty and destructive thing to do. This book you are now reading, alas, is an exemplification of this destructiveness. Even in its celebration of literature's magic, it suspends that magic by bringing it into the open.

Two motives may be identified for this effort of demystification. One is the way literary study, for the most part institutionalized in schools and universities, to a lesser degree in journalism, is part of the general penchant of our culture toward getting knowledge for its own sake. Western universities are dedicated to finding out the truth about everything, as in the motto of Harvard University: "Veritas." This includes the truth about literature. In my own case, a vocation for literary study was a displacement of a vocation for science. I shifted from physics to literature in the middle of my undergraduate study. My motive was a quasi-scientific curiosity about what seemed to me at that point (and still does) the radical strangeness of literary works, their difference from one another and from ordinary everyday uses of language. What in the world, I asked myself, could have led Tennyson, presumably a sane man, to use language in such an exceedingly peculiar way? Why did he do that? What conceivable use did such language use have when it was written, or could it have today? I wanted, and still want, to account for literature in the same way as physicists want to account for anomalous "signals" coming from around a black hole or from a quasar. I am still trying, and still puzzled.

The other motive is apotropaic. This is a noble or ignoble motive, depending on how you look at it. People have a healthy fear of the power literary works have to instill what may be dangerous or unjust assumptions about race, gender, or class. Both cultural studies and rhetorical reading, the latter especially in its "deconstructive" mode, have this hygienic or defensive purpose. By the time a rhetorical reading, or a "slow reading," has shown the mechanism by which literary magic works, that magic no longer works. It is seen as a kind of hocus-pocus. By the time a feminist reading of *Paradise Lost* has been performed, Milton's sexist assumptions ("Hee for God only, shee for God in him.") have been shown for what they are. The poem, however, has also lost its marvelous ability to present to the reader an imaginary Eden inhabited by two beautiful and eroticized people: "So hand in hand they passed, the lovliest pair/That ever since in loves embraces met." The demystified reader may also have been reminded by the implacable critic that this Edenic vision is presented through the eyes of a resentful and envious witness, Satan. "O Hell!," says Satan, "what doe mine eyes with grief behold."

Milton's Satan might be called the prototypical demystifier, or suspicious reader, the critic as sceptic or disbeliever. Or the prototype of the modern critical reader might be Friedrich Nietzsche. Nietzsche was trained as a professor of ancient rhetoric. His *The Genealogy of Morals*, along with much other writing by him, is a work of cultural criticism before the fact. In a famous statement in "On Truth and Lie in an Extra-Moral Sense," Nietzsche defines truth, "veritas," not as a statement or representation of things as they are, but as a tropological fabrication, in short, as literature. "Truth," says Nietzsche, "is a mobile army of metaphors, metonymies, and anthropo-morphisms." The reader will note that Nietzsche sees cultural forms, including literature, as warlike, aggressive, a "mobile army" that must be resisted by equally warlike weapons wielded by the critic. The reader will also note that Nietzsche gives an example of this by using an anthropomorphism of his own in calling truth a mobile army. He turns truth's own weapon against itself.

No doubt about it, these two forms of critical reading, rhetorical reading and cultural studies, have contributed to the death of literature. It is no accident that critical reading as demystification arose in exacerbated forms at just the time literature's sovereign power for cultural indoctrination was beginning to fade. We no longer so much want, or are willing, to be bamboozled by literature.

WHY I LOVED *THE SWISS FAMILY ROBINSON*

I return now to *The Swiss Family Robinson*. I shall use it to exemplify the uneasy co-presence of the two kinds of reading I have defined. I have just re-read this novel, almost sixty-five years after my last reading, to see what I make of it now. I must confess that I have been as enchanted, or almost, as I was at my first reading, at about the age of ten. I can still see that tree house in my mind's eye, the one the Robinson family builds after being shipwrecked. I have rediscovered again that wonderful, safely uninhabited, tropical island, teeming with every sort of bird, beast, fish, tree, and plant. I can still see the fully developed farm the Robinson family constructs, with a winter house and a summer house, farm buildings, fields of potatoes, rice, cassava, vegetable and flower gardens, fruit trees, fences, aqueducts, all sorts of domesticated animals multiplying like anything – ducks, geese, ostriches, cattle, pigs, pigeons, dogs, a tame jackal, tame flamingos (!), and so on. You name it, they have got it in abundance – plenty of sugar, salt, flour, rice, utensils, even farm machinery. I still rejoice in the decision the father, mother, and two of the children make at the end to stay in their colony of "New Switzerland," even when they are rescued and could go back to "civilization."

I think I know now, however, just why I found *The Swiss Family Robinson* so enchanting. One of my earliest memories is of being carried in a "pack basket" on my father's back on a camping trip with the rest of my family and another family to the Adirondack Mountains in northern New York State. Camping out was for me magical in the same way that reading *The Swiss Family Robinson* was magical. Equipped with no more than you could carry on your back, you could "set up camp," cut some fragrant balsam boughs for bedding, make a camp fire for cooking and heat, and, in short, create a whole new domestic world in the wilderness. I can still remember the pleasure of falling asleep in the open-fronted lean-to with the other children, wrapped in my blanket (no sleeping bags then), smelling the balsam, and listening to the murmur of the adults' voices as they sat by the dying campfire. *The Swiss Family Robinson* is a hyperbolic version of that pleasure. It is a deep satisfaction of the nest-making instinct. It is the creation, out of the materials at hand (plus a few things saved from the wreck, of course!), of a new world, a metaworld. In this, *The*

Swiss Family Robinson is a marvelous allegory of what I am claiming every literary work does. Within the story the family creates a new realm, with hard work and ingenuity. The reader of the book creates within his or her imagination a new realm. This is a virtual reality that for the time seems more real, and certainly more worthy to be lived in, than the "real world."

READING *THE SWISS FAMILY ROBINSON LENTO*

So much for the *allegro* reading – the *lento* reading, the suspicious reading, produces something very different. Almost sixty-five years of training and professional practice have made me unable to suspend my habits of critical reading. I would certainly not have been able to perform the *lento* reading at the age of ten, nor would I have wanted to. Evidence of that resistance is my annoyance when my mother told me the work is a fiction and pointed out the author's name on the title page. It was the beginning of a break in the magic.

This fictitious, factitious quality is rubbed in, unnecessarily, it seems to me, by a gratuitous disclaimer on the verso of the title page of one paperback copy of *The Swiss Family Robinson* I have procured: "This is a work of fiction. All the characters and events portrayed in the book are fictitious, and any resemblance to real people or events is purely coincidental." Why bother to say that? Who but an innocent child of ten, such as I was, would think *The Swiss Family Robinson* is anything but a work of fiction? Who in the world would think at this late date of suing Tor Books for giving away secrets about real people in a book first published, in the original German version, in 1812? Moreover, the disclaimer, it happens, as is so often the case, is a lie. The father, mother, and four sons of the Swiss Family Robinson are closely modeled, so we are told, on the family of the author, Johann David Wyss. Wyss was a Swiss clergyman and sometime army chaplain. He lived, as I noted in Chapter 1, from 1743 to 1818. Ernst, the second son in the story, is, for example, modeled on Wyss's son, Johann Rudolf Wyss. That son, with his father's concurrence, prepared the lengthy manuscript for publication and made many changes in it.

I was right in one way at least. *The Swiss Family Robinson*, as English readers know it today, has no single author. It is a composite work, as well as being a translation. It began as improvised evening stories that Johann David Wyss told to his four sons. These new stories were a follow-up to reading Defoe's *Robinson Crusoe* aloud to them in the evening. Wyss, though of large girth, was an avid hunter, fisherman, and outdoorsman, a genuine Swiss. He also had read many travel books (Captain Cook's *Voyages*, Lord Anson's circumnavigation of 1748, and many others). He knew a lot of natural history, much of it clearly from books with illustrations – of kangaroos, flamingos, platypuses, and so on.

Wyss was a true son of the Enlightenment. The stories were a pleasurable way to teach his sons natural history and what might be called "woodsy lore," for example how to build a rustic bridge, or how to calculate the height of a tree from the ground, or how to cure an animal hide. His goal, Wyss said, was "to awaken the curiosity of my sons by interesting observations, to leave time for the activity of their imagination, and then to correct any error they might fall into." Wyss wrote down many of the episodes of the endlessly extendable story in a bulky manuscript of 841 pages. Johann Rudolf Wyss, one of Johann David Wyss's sons, was a philosophy professor at Berne, a folklorist, and author of the Swiss national anthem. With his father's approval, he revised and organized the manuscript for publication, under his own (Johann Rudolf's) name, in 1812. It was called *Der Schweizerische Robinson; oder, Der schiffbruchige Schweizerprediger und seine Familie* (*The Swiss Family Robinson; or, the Shipwrecked Swiss Clergyman and His Family*).

That is not the end of the story, however. A French translation by one Mme la Baronne Isabelle de Montolieu, with a new ending, was published in 1814. Another French translation, by Mme Elise Volart, with yet new material, followed. The first English translation, *The Family Robinson Crusoe*, was made by Mary Jane Godwin, with more new material. It was published by M. J. Godwin and Co. in 1814. Mary Jane Godwin may have used the first French translation rather than the German original. She was the wife of the political philosopher, novelist, and educationist, William Godwin. The book was part of William Godwin's children's book project, "the juvenile library." The preface, which sounds as if it might have beem written by William Godwin himself, is actually Johann Rudolf Wyss's explanation of how he came to make a publishable book out of his father's manuscripts. Nevertheless, the preface is, as Jason Wohlstadter has observed, a good expression of William Godwin's anti-Rousseauistic claim that children can be taught much natural history, geography, and other useful things by books like *The Family Robinson Crusoe*.

Many new English versions followed. New episodes continued to be added, and abbreviated versions were produced. The concluding episode of the rescue of Jenny Montrose, the castaway English girl, is, for example, missing from the earliest versions, for example the Godwin one. The story is in principle endless, like a television soap opera, always inviting the interpolation of yet another episode, the encounter with yet another exotic animal, tree, or bird. The English version by W. H. G. Kingston (1889) has tended to become standard for English readers. I have no knowledge of which version I read, since the book has not survived among the books from my childhood. I do, however, have my old copy of *Alice in Wonderland* and *Through the Looking-Glass*, with the Tenniel illustrations. I taught myself to read that book at the age of five or six. I was tired of depending on my mother to read the book to me. Though neither I nor my mother knew it, this was in defiance of a prohibition expressed in the preface to the Godwin translation of what they called the *The Family Robinson Crusoe*:

> In reality, it is very rarely, and perhaps never, proper that children should read by themselves; few indeed are the individuals in those tender years that are not either too indolent, too lively, or too capricious to employ themselves usefully upon this species of occupation.

What is most interesting, for my purposes here, is the way reader after reader has been so taken by the virtual reality *The Swiss Family Robinson* reveals that he or she feels authorized to extend the original with new episodes. It seems as if, once you are inside this alternative world, you can explore and record even those parts of it Wyss did not happen to write down, so powerful is the reader's persuasion of its independent existence.

How to Read Comparatively, or
Playing the Mug's Game

Six

BEFORE AND AFTER *THE SWISS FAMILY ROBINSON*

What is tendentious or ideological about *The Swiss Family Robinson* (1812)? What is noticed by the wise, demystified, critical reader I have become? A comparison with two other works, Daniel Defoe's *Robinson Crusoe* (1719), in one historical direction, and the Alice books (1865 and 1871), in the other, with a further gesture toward the quite recent *Foe* (1986), by the South African author J. M. Coetzee, will allow economical answers.

Robinson Crusoe is a version of the prodigal son story. It depends on the ironic disjunction between the first-person narrator then and the wiser first-person narrator now, just as I am second-guessing my naiveté in being taken in by *The Swiss Family Robinson*. The irony in *Robinson Crusoe* works both ways. The older, wiser narrator tells the reader what a self-destructive fool he was not to obey his father and stay at home to become prosperous in the middle station to which Providence has called him. At the same time the reader knows there would be no story to tell if Crusoe had not disobeyed his father and gone to sea. The reader, not so secretly, admires Crusoe's foolhardiness, as well as his courage and cleverness in saving himself when he is shipwrecked. After all, Crusoe's shipwreck is ultimately the occasion of his conversion experience. The novel, seen this way, becomes ironic praise of self-help, independence, and self-reliance. Irony of this sort is more or less completely absent from *The Swiss Family Robinson*.

Alice's Adventures in Wonderland and *Through the Looking-Glass*, in the other historical direction, already anticipate modernist and postmodernist anxieties about the constructed nature of selfhood, its dependence on the language of other people. The Alice books also present a modernist notion about the impossibility of making sense, on the basis of traditional assumptions, of an absurd, incongruous, even downright crazy, world. The Alice books are also quintessentially "literature" in their dependence on wordplay, on allusion and parody, and on an ironic discrepancy between what the narrator knows and what the heroine knows, wise child though she is. These features are carried to the point of overt nonsense, as every reader of these books knows. An enormous and still mounting secondary literature has grown up around both *Robinson Crusoe* and the Alice books, but relatively little has been written about *The Swiss Family Robinson*. This is probably because no one but specialists in children's literature, for the most part, have taken it seriously enough to reflect on it.

FOE AS REVISIONIST COMMENTARY

Coetzee's *Foe* is the latest (so far as I know), and one of the greatest, of the many "Robinsoniads" that Defoe's *Robinson Crusoe* has generated. Just as readers of *The Swiss Family Robinson* have been inspired to add further episodes to the original, so readers of *Robinson Crusoe* have been inspired to write entirely new books, such as *The Swiss Family Robinson* and *Foe*. *Foe* imagines an entirely different narrative about "Cruso's" island. A shortening of Defoe's name and Crusoe's indicates the violence

How to Read Comparatively

Coetzee is doing to the original. This is a mutilation like that Friday has suffered, in *Foe*.

The chief narrator of *Foe* is a female castaway, Susan Barton. She swims ashore on Cruso's island. She finds Cruso there with a Friday whose tongue has been cut out by slave traders, so that he is mute. That mutilation corresponds to another "yet more hideous mutilation" Susan glimpses when, late in the novel, she sees him dancing naked, except for a flying robe. Or the reader may think she sees another mutilation. Her report is slightly ambiguous: "What had been hidden from me," she says, "was revealed. I saw; or, I should say, my eyes were opened to what was present to them. I saw and believed I had seen . . ." Just what she saw is not revealed to the reader. Friday, in any case, dwells in silence. He cannot tell his own story. That means we are free to make up any story we like about him. He responds only to a few commands Cruso has taught him.

Almost everything is different on the island in *Foe* from what it is in Defoe's version. Foe's Cruso has saved only a knife from the wreck, not a whole collection of useful things. Cruso, Friday, and Susan must subsist on a bitter lettuce, fish, and birds' eggs. Cruso, absurdly, with slave-labor help from Friday, is building an elaborate system of stone-walled terraces, even though he has no seed to plant there. All three are rescued after a year and taken back to London, There Susan seeks out "Foe," a famous author, to get him to write her story in a truthful way, since she feels incapable of doing so herself.

Much of the latter half of this short novel consists of reflections by Susan, alone or in dialogue with Foe. These mostly have to do with the nature of narrative and with the difficulties of writing a truthful one. One thread in this strand makes *Foe* another example supporting my conviction that literature gives access to a virtual reality. Susan imagines Foe writing away in his attic, then stopping, leaving his imaginary characters, grenadiers, thieves, whores, and the rest, momentarily frozen in the world of shades from which he summons them with his pen. "He has turned his mind from us, I told myself," Susan writes to Foe, during a time she is separated from him, while he is hiding out to avoid being arrested for debt. Foe, she thinks, has turned his mind away from her and Friday, "as easily as if we were two of his grenadiers in Flanders, forgetting that while his grenadiers fall into an enchanted sleep whenever he absents himself, Friday and I continue to eat and drink and fret."

Susan appeals to Foe to turn her truthful story into a narrative. She wants a story that is not only true, but that also has substance:

> For though my story gives the truth, it does not give the substance of the truth (I see that clearly, we need not pretend it is otherwise). To tell the truth in all its substance you must have quiet, and a comfortable chair away from all distraction, and a window to stare through; and then the knack of seeing waves when there are fields before your eyes, and of feeling the tropic sun when it is cold; and at your fingertips the words with which to capture the vision before it fades. I have none of these, while you have all.

The Coetzeean twist to the idea that literature gives access to an alternative world is to suggest by the invaginations (Derrida's word) of narrative within narrative, as well as by overt statement, that the real world too is a virtual reality. Coetzee's *Foe* is a reading of *Robinson Crusoe* in many different ways. One of these readings is the implication that it was a pack of lies made up by Defoe. Susan's written narrative, on the contrary, tells what really happened. It reveals what Defoe should have written down, if he cared for the truth. Her narrative, however, is framed by an account of her encounter with a man named "Foe." I suppose the pun on "foe" as enemy is intended. An author is enemy to the truth. Foe's life and writings in many ways correspond to those of the historical person, Daniel Defoe. Foe is, for example, writing what appears to be *A Journal of the Plague Year* and has written the "True Relation of the Apparition of one Mrs Veal," real works by Daniel Defoe. Outside Susan's narration of encounters with Foe is a brief final section in the first-person present tense. This is narrated by an unnamed additional narrator, Coetzee himself or some impersonal narrative voice.

The adept reader, however, at a certain moment realizes that the frame story, the story of Susan's adventures within it, and the final narration by yet another "I" are three more packs of lies made up by Coetzee. This vertiginous doubling has a way of including the reader's world in the turnings inside out. The reader wonders whether his or her real world may not be a virtual reality too. This fear is expressed directly by Foe. "Let us confront our worst fear," he says,

> which is that we have all of us been called into the world from a different order (which we have now forgotten) by a conjurer unknown to us . . . Do we of necessity become puppets in a story whose end is invisible to us, and towards which we are marched like condemned felons?

A little later Foe thinks of this as the experience (or rather non-experience, since we could not experience it as such), of being written into existence by God, just as, the reader might reflect, Susan, Cruso, Friday, and Foe have been written into existence by Coetzee:

> We are accustomed to believe that our world was created by God speaking the Word; but I ask, may it not rather be that he wrote it, wrote a Word so long we have yet to come to the end of it? May it not be that God continually writes the world, the world and all that is in it?

To which Susan replies: "As to God's writing, my opinion is: If he writes, he employs a secret writing, which it is not given to us, who are part of that writing, to read."

Coetzee's *Foe*, in a final twist to my idea that literature invokes a virtual reality, opposes two forms of storytelling. One is the shapely Aristotlean narrative with a beginning, middle, and end. Foe proposes at one point to turn Susan's life into such a narrative, in response to her appeal to him to give her life's true story substance:

> It is thus that we make up a book: loss, then quest, then recovery; beginning, then middle, then end. As to novelty, this is lent by the island episode – which is properly the second part of the middle – and by the reversal in which the daughter takes up the quest abandoned by her mother.

The latter reference is to the part of Susan's story that has to do with her search for her lost daughter in Brazil and with the appearance of a woman in London who claims to be that lost daughter. About this motif there would be much to say, but I defer the saying.

Susan is dismayed by Foe's neat proposal. She responds by saying that the lack Foe senses in her narrative is a silence at its center, the silence of Friday's muteness. Every true story, Foe and Susan go on later in the novel to agree, has an inaccessible silence at its center. This is somewhat like that silence of the Sirens about which Blanchot writes. "In every story," says Foe, "there is a silence, some sight concealed, some word unspoken, I believe. Till we have spoken the unspoken we have not come to the heart of the story." To which Susan replies: "It is for us to open Friday's mouth and hear what it holds: silence, perhaps, or a roar, like the roar of a seashell held to the ear." Foe responds: "We must make Friday's silence speak, as well as the silence surrounding Friday."

Early in the novel, Susan writes of decisive moments in our lives as the instantaneous interventions of "chance." This is certainly different from Crusoe's belief, in Defoe's novel, that a Providence watches over every event in his life. "What are these blinks of an eyelid," asks Susan, "against which the only defence is an eternal and inhuman wakefulness? Might they not be the cracks and chinks through which another voice, other voices, speak in our lives?" These other voices come from the central unspoken silence that is, for Coetzee, the motive and determining force of every story. In the last section the anonymous "I" descends toward that center, figured as the sunken ship that brought Friday and Cruso to the island.

It might seem that Foe's salient features make it a characteristic postmodern work: the intricacies of narration that turn reality and fiction inside out; the parodistic irony directed against a source text; the repetitions with a difference of the same haunting phrase in different contexts ("With a sigh, making barely a splash, I slipped overboard."); the genre-breaking overt reflections on the question of storytelling that make Foe a work of literary theory as well as a novel; a putting in question of literary history, of history tout court, of biography and autobiography; the suspension of referential or "realist" models of storytelling; the forceful putting in doubt of the reader's own stabilities and certainties, so that he or she fears to be dreaming when awake. It might seem that *Foe* is "typically" postmodern, that is, if one forgets that these narrational intricacies are already present in Cervantes's *Don Quixote*, or that both for Calderón in Renaissance Spain and for Lewis Carroll in Victorian England, not to speak of Shakespeare, "Life is a dream." "We are such stuff/As dreams are made on," says Prospero in *The Tempest*.

LITERATURE AND INTELLECTUAL HISTORY

My juxtaposition of *The Swiss Family Robinson*, *Robinson Crusoe*, the Alice books, and *Foe* must not be misunderstood. I do not see them as dots on a line representing some all-inclusive, ineluctable, historical progression from the time of George I, for *Crusoe*, to the period of Romanticism, for *The Swiss Family Robinson*, to the high Victorian period for the Alice books, to our own times for *Foe*. No doubt these books are of their own times. Much in them can be explained by their historical placement. They can, however, hardly be said to be "typical" of their times and places. Each of these works is atypical. It is not typical of anything but itself.

Is any work, moreover, really "typical of its period?" *The Swiss Family Robinson*, for example, is coeval with German romanticism and German idealist philosophy. It is contemporary with the Schlegel brothers, with Hegel, Hölderlin, and Novalis in Germany, not to speak of Goethe's *Elective Affinities* (1809). *The Swiss Family Robinson* is also coeval with English romanticism, with Wordsworth, Coleridge, Keats, and Shelley in England, along with Jane Austen. Connecting Wyss's work with these worthies in a search for similarities does not get one very far. Nor is Defoe all that much like Swift and Pope, nor Carroll's work like, say, Tennyson, whose *Maud* is hilariously caricatured in the talking flowers episode of *Through the Looking-Glass*: " 'She's coming!' cried the Larkspur. 'I hear her footstep, thump, thump, along the gravel-walk.' " Coetzee's work has its own unique stamp. It is not just "postmodernist." Each of these works fits my definition of a literary work as incomparable, singular, strange. None is satisfactorily explicable either by its historical placement or by its author's biography. My juxtapositions are intended to show how that is the case especially for *The Swiss Family Robinson*.

One intellectual context, however, is useful for understanding *The Swiss Family Robinson*. It is no accident that William Godwin's wife made the first English translation of it. William Godwin was, among other things, an educational theorist. As Jason Wohlstadter has shown in detail, he was deeply influenced by Jean-Jacques Rousseau's *Émile*, though he differed from Rousseau on some points. Godwin wrote theories of childhood education. He also wrote and published children's books, for example his own *Fables Ancient and Modern* (1805). The latter was brought out under the pseudonym of "Edward Baldwin." The Godwins must have seen in Wyss's novel a confirmation of their theories. Like Rousseau, and like Godwin, Wyss evidently believed that the best way to learn is not from books but directly from nature. The children in *The Swiss Family Robinson*, Émile-like, learn about kangaroos, sharks, whales, jackals, lions, rubber trees, cassava, and so on, not from books but through direct encounter with these beasts and plants. The irony of course is that Johann David Wyss was teaching his children about these things through words and pictures, not through things. The reader of *The Swiss Family Robinson* also learns through reading, not through direct encounters with nature. Wyss had presumably never seen a live platypus in his life.

As opposed to the ironic undercutting of himself by Crusoe's first-person narrator, the first-person narrator of The Swiss Family Robinson, the father, is without regrets or self-irony. He is, on the contrary, rather self-congratulatory and self-approving. No doubts exist about the identity of the characters in Wyss's story. They have fixed personalities from the beginning. These personalities are carefully labeled: Fritz's courage and level-headedness as the eldest, Ernst's laziness and bookish thoughtfulness in the next eldest son, then the impetuous and somewhat foolhardy Jack, and, last, the youngest, the naïve but game Franz.

Wyss's motive seems to have been partly to write a book that would correct Robinson Crusoe, just as Coetzee's Foe was quite overtly to do in our own epoch. The Swiss Family Robinson is the most famous and best of the "Robinsoniads" that followed the original in the eighteenth and early nineteenth centuries. The two adjectives in the title, "Swiss" and "family" identify what is being corrected. In place of Robinson Crusoe's isolated self-reliance, it puts the "family values" of loving interdependence and cooperation, along with the pieties of nationalism. The Swiss Family Robinson is unashamedly sexist and patriarchal. The father is explicitly referred to with the latter adjective. The long-suffering mother is kept in her place, cheerfully performing endless household chores. She has no given name. She is just "die Mütter," or sometimes she is called by the diminutive "Mütterchen." Any other females are conspicuously absent, until the climactic episode of Jenny Montrose, added later. These boys can go it alone, without any women around, except the mother, who sews, cooks, and washes. Girls may like The Swiss Family Robinson, but it is not a "girls' book," unless all that housework done by the mother can be seen as useful instructions about a woman's lot.

In place of Crusoe's faithful/faithless, ironically undercut, English Puritanism, *The Swiss Family Robinson* puts a Swiss Protestantism that is never disobeyed or questioned. That Protestantism stresses piety, hard work, and collective rather than individual self-help. A great deal of praying punctuates *The Swiss Family Robinson*. That is something I had entirely forgotten from my first reading, perhaps because my father too was a clergyman, a Baptist minister. We had grace before meals and were taught to say prayers before going to sleep. It probably seemed natural enough to me that there is a lot of praying in this book. The difference from *Robinson Crusoe* is that in *The Swiss Family Robinson* religion is much more nominal, taken for granted, incorporated in everyday behavior. Defoe's *Robinson Crusoe* is, among other things, a fictive Puritan conversion narrative, modeled on real seventeenth-century ones. A Puritan Protestant interpretation of experience is deeply inwrought in *Robinson Crusoe*. It is much harder to miss or pass over than the routine praying in *The Swiss Family Robinson*. An example is a lengthy reflection by Crusoe about the "secret intimations of Providence" that have led him to make right decisions when the wrong would have been disastrous: "certainly they are a proof of the converse of spirits and the secret communication between those embodied and those unembodied, and such a proof as can never be withstood," and so on.

The ultimate message of *Robinson Crusoe*, however, is ambiguous. While Crusoe is camping out for twenty-eight years, two months, and nineteen days on his desert island and having his conversion experience, the slave-worked sugar and tobacco plantation he has left behind in "the Brazils" is flourishing. Crusoe ends his life a rich man, whereas Coetzee's Cruso dies in Susan's arms on the way back to England after they are rescued. Defoe's Crusoe's wealth is another example of Providence's care for him. He also maintains possession of the island he had lived on for so many years. He colonizes it successfully. This endpoint is a spectacular example of "religion and the rise of capitalism," to borrow the title of a famous book by R. H. Tawney. It also anticipates the ending of *The Swiss Family Robinson*. In the latter book too a permanent colony is established.

Both *Robinson Crusoe* and *The Swiss Family Robinson* are episodic and open-ended, promising further adventures that might be told. Defoe did publish *The Farther Adventures of Robinson Crusoe* a few months after the publication of *Robinson Crusoe* in 1719. *The Serious Reflections . . . of Robinson Crusoe* appeared in 1720. Both *Robinson Crusoe* and the two Alice books, however, have plots. All three have narrative goals toward which the whole story moves, however wild those may be in the Alice books, each of which has its ending in a scene of surrealist violence. "You're nothing but a pack of cards!" cries Alice in *Alice's Adventures*, and they turn into just that: "the whole pack rose up into the air, and came flying down upon her." The last episode of *Through the Looking-Glass* is that weird dinner party in which Alice is introduced to the leg of mutton and then to the pudding: "Alice – Mutton: Mutton – Alice . . . Pudding – Alice: Alice – Pudding." When Alice wakes from her dream, the Red Queen turns back into the black kitten. *The Swiss Family Robinson*, on the contrary, is endlessly episodic. In each episode, each one probably corresponding to a single evening's improvisation in the original oral version, the family confronts some new problem or other. They then learn something about science or natural history from it, for example how to make a kayak, or pemmican, or what a kangaroo is and how to kill and skin one. They then wait for the next adventure. No reason can be given for these ever to end. The ending in the family's rescue seems more or less accidental and unmotivated.

The central purpose of The Swiss Family Robinson is to teach natural history. One by one the animals, birds, and fish the family encounters are named out of the storehouse of Father Robinson's knowledge, just as Adam named all the animals, in Genesis. God is praised for his benevolence and wisdom in creating all these living things. The bones of whales and birds, for example, are said to be hollow to make the creatures lighter: "The bones of birds are also hollow, for the same reason, and in all this we see conspicuously the wisdom and goodness of the great Creator." The tamed creatures are given pet names by the children, Hurricane for the ostrich, Fangs and Coco for two tame jackals, Knips for the tame monkey, Storm for the buffalo bull they make into a beast of burden, Lightfoot for the "onager," and so on. All this naming firmly incorporates these creatures into civilized society.

VIOLENCE IN *THE SWISS FAMILY ROBINSON*

The Swiss Family Robinson's episodes recount the gradual taming of a wilderness. The island is transformed into a thriving domain of farms, houses, gardens, fields, and pens. Wild animals that are encountered must either be shot or tamed, sometimes some of each. An example is the encounter with a troop of monkeys, one of whom becomes a pet after they shoot the mother. The ostrich encounter, the kangaroo encounter, and the eagle encounter tell the same story with different materials. I had forgotten how much murdering of innocent wildlife exists in this novel. The instinct, or learned behavior, of the father and his four sons, when some animal or bird or fish appears before them, is to shoot it or to spear it. Fish are for catching and eating. Animals and birds are for shooting and eating, if they are edible. Reading the book again after so long, I found all this mayhem shocking, offensive to my green piety. Emphasis, however, is placed on killing animals cleanly, so they do not suffer long, and on not killing them unnecessarily, though a lot of that occurs anyhow.

The ideology of hunting and using guns in *The Swiss Family Robinson* is more or less the same as the one I was taught by my Virginia farm-bred father, grandfathers, and uncles, except that an irresponsibly small amount of safety instruction is given in Wyss's novel. I too was taught to kill only for food, not for sheer sport, though I could not bring myself to kill anything now, unless I were starving to death. I was also taught, however: "Don't ever point a gun at yourself or at another person"; "Assume every gun is loaded, even if you have unloaded it yourself fifteen minutes ago"; "Don't leave loaded guns around the house"; "Store ammunition separately, in a locked place." My father showed me a hole in the paneling of the living room in my Grandfather Miller's farmhouse. It had been been made, he said, by a bullet from a supposedly unloaded gun. The Robinson boys are taught none of this, at least the reader is not told that they are. They wander around, often on their own, hyperbolically trigger-happy, blasting away at anything that moves.

What is the function of all this violence? This question returns me to what I said in the first chapter about the irruptive violence of literary works' beginnings as proleptic of a violence within the works themselves. The violence of killing in chapter after chapter of *The Swiss Family Robinson* enacts, in however muted and covert a way, that drama of sacrificial violence Nietzsche saw as essential to all art. In many chapters the Swiss family encounters some strange and threatening animal, bird, or fish: sharks, buffaloes, elephants, walruses, ostriches, jackals, lions, a tiger, a ferocious hyena. In each case the creature, or more than one among many of them, is shot, identified, skinned, or taken home to be eaten, or stuffed for the museum, in a somewhat comic enactment of the progress of enlightened civilization.

One killing, however, is not enough. The threatening outside of civilization's small enclosure has to be confronted again and again in different forms. Fear of the outside, which *The Swiss Family Robinson* both generated and appeased in me as a child, has to be faced down again and again, potentially *ad infinitum*. If a superabundance of food in various forms is present for the Robinsons, so also is an inexhaustible supply of wild and dangerous things, all demanding to be killed or tamed, but without hope of ever coming to the end of them.

This mechanism of the arousal of fear and its always partial appeasement may explain why reading a single literary work is never enough. The person who is hooked on reading always needs one more virtual reality. No one of them ever fully succeeds in doing its work. Habitual readers of mystery stories will know what I mean. They will also know that this arousal of fear, and its always only partial appeasement, are intensely pleasurable. Mystery stories give great pleasure, but they do not wholly satisfy. You always need to read another. Another murder always remains to be solved, perhaps one committed unwittingly by yourself, as Oedipus killed Laius without knowing Laius was his father.

The wildness of *The Swiss Family Robinson*, the endless proliferation of its episodes, and the excessive killing that occurs within it, are matched by the irrationality of Crusoe's self-condemnation, a spiritual violence that runs through the book. That self-accusation condemns traits that make him in the end a rich imperialist, living off slave labor. The wildness of The Swiss Family Robinson is matched also by the wild illogic of dreams in the Alice books. Freud said we dream in order not to wake up. Some dreams, however, are so violent and so terrifying that they do wake us up. The silent center that may be a roar, hidden in the heart of every story, is Coetzee's version of literature's irrationality. Literature's wildness, source of the intense pleasure it gives, both allows us to keep dreaming within the ideological constants of the culture to which we belong and, at the same time, wakes us up from what James Joyce, notoriously, called "the nightmare of history."

Fortunately, for the Swiss family if not for the creatures already on their island when they arrive, a great store of powder and shot, along with many other essentials of Swiss farm civilization, have been saved from the wreck: a cow, a donkey, a pig, ducks, chickens, fruit trees, knives, guns, a Bible of course, a good many other books, and so on. This is because the ship was bound for Australia, apparently, to found a colony there. It was loaded with the materials necessary for colonizing. In Coetzee's Foe, on the contrary, "Cruso" has, as I have mentioned, swum ashore with nothing saved but a single knife, whereas Crusoe, in Defoe's novel, salvages all sorts of useful things from the wreck. The account of the library saved from the ship in The Swiss Family Robinson is a more or less overt indication of its "sources":

> Besides a variety of books of voyages, travels, divinity, and
> natural history (several containing fine colored illustrations),
> there were histories and scientific works, as well as standard

fiction in several languages. There was also a good
assortment of maps, charts, mathematical and astronomical
instruments, and an excellent pair of globes.

Why the Robinsons do not use these maps and instruments
to determine just where they are, and on what island, is never
explained. This is no doubt because it is a fundamental feature
of the story that they not know where they are, nor even the
full size and contours of their island. Robinson Crusoe, on the
contrary takes full measure of his smaller island, as does
Coetzee's Cruso. *Robinson Crusoe* is mentioned explicitly twice
in *The Swiss Family Robinson*, as well as named explicitly as a
model in that original preface, present in the Godwin version
but not in the later ones in print today. Though it takes some
enterprise to rescue so many things from what remains of the
wreck, nevertheless their availability tips the balance in the
Swiss family's favor, as also happens for Robinson Crusoe. In
both cases, the basic materials of European civilization are
brought ashore, flamboyantly so in *The Swiss Family Robinson*.

THE CRUSOE BOOKS AND IMPERIALISM

Since Wyss's goal was to teach his children natural history, he
notoriously jumbled together animals, fish, and plants from
all over the world on this one tropical island, in absurd co-
presence: penguins, jackals, hyenas, elephants, kangaroos,
bears, buffaloes, lions, tigers, a boa constrictor, salmon, seals,
walruses, whales, sturgeon, herring, ducks and pigeons of
every sort, quails, partridges, antelopes, rabbits, honey bees,
potatoes, rice, Indian corn (maize), cassava, vanilla, coconuts,
calabashes, rubber trees, cotton bushes, figs, and so on, a
virtually endless list.

Besides killing and eating, or taming, the creatures they

encounter, the Swiss family does one more very eighteenth-century thing with them. Museums, as well as encyclopedias, were an important feature of the Enlightenment. The Robinson family gradually collect in a museum at their "Rockburg" dwelling specimens they have preserved and stuffed. Taxidermy is another of the arts the father teaches his children. These specimens include a stuffed condor, the giant boa constrictor, and many other victims.

Wyss's "New Switzerland" is an Edenic world of profusion, of plenitude. It is a world swarming with things to be shot, tamed, or eaten, or farmed and then eaten, if you are clever enough to know how to do so, as in this description of the results of all the family's vegetable garden labor:

> Fortunately, in this beautiful climate little or no attention was necessary to our kitchen garden, the seeds sprang up and flourished without apparently the slightest regard for the time or season of the year. Peas, beans, wheat, barley, rye, and Indian corn seemed constantly ripe, while cucumbers, melons, and all sorts of other vegetables grew luxuriantly.

Poor Cruso, in Coetzee's *Foe*, by contrast, has, you will remember, no seeds. I found all the abundance in *The Swiss Family Robinson* and all the descriptions of eating (even eating odd things like kangaroo meat) wonderfully reassuring when I was a child. This book, plus early camping experiences and some actual knowledge about the woods, has left me still with the belief, no doubt only partly true, that I would be able to survive all right, thank you, in the woods, at least for a while. I would survive especially if I had some company, though perhaps not quite so splendidly as does the Swiss Family Robinson.

Robinson Crusoe, on the contrary, stresses the difficulty and precariousness of going it alone in a wilderness. With a few exceptions, Crusoe is not sure of the names of any of the animals, birds, and plants on his island, nor which are useful, nor how to use them. He has great difficulty getting his few grains of wheat and rice to germinate. Whatever Crusoe does, he does with great effort, with much trial and error, and with many failures. His life is, in Hobbes's words, "nasty," "solitary," and "brutish," if not "short." Crusoe stresses

> the exceeding laboriousness of my work; the many hours which for want of tools, want of help, and want of skill everything I did took up out of my time. For example, I was full two and forty days making me a board for a long shelf, which I wanted in my cave . . . My next concern was to get me a stone mortar to stamp or beat some corn in; for as to the mill, there was no thought of arriving to that perfection of art with one pair of hands. To supply this want I was at a great loss; for of all trades in the world I was as perfectly unqualified for a stone-cutter as for any whatever; neither had I any tools to go about it with.

Coetzee's *Foe* makes this helplessness hyperbolic.

Robinson Crusoe responded to another American myth I had been taught, the belief that if you were lost and alone in the wilderness you would have a hard time of it, but might possibly survive if you were brave, resourceful, and lucky. In the United States today versions of that myth are still active in survival tales dramatized in books, films, and on television. In contrast to *Robinson Crusoe*, the Swiss family Robinson know the names of everything they find on their island, what each thing is good for, and how to do everything needful. It is as though Wyss were deliberately responding to *Robinson Crusoe* by saying, in effect: "A good Swiss family with rural experience and knowledge of natural history would fare immeasurably better in the wilderness than this maladroit urban Englishman. I'll show you how."

The Swiss Family Robinson, finally, is a relatively early example of colonial or imperialist literature. This is so in a way different from *Robinson Crusoe*. The latter blandly endorses slavery, for example, and sees South American natives as all cannibal savages in need of conversion to Protestantism. Spanish conquistadores, however, are condemned by Crusoe for being Catholic and for their indiscriminate slaughter of indigenous South Americans. The Swiss Robinsons, however, recreate on their desert island, without any interference from "savages," a nearly exact replica of Swiss rural culture. Their plantation is spoken of several times toward the end of the book as a "dominion" or "colony." They name this colony "New Switzerland" (like "New England" in the United States). They decide, even after they are rescued, to stay there, to remain in charge of their colony, to enlarge it, to add more people to it, and to make it more and more an outpost of Swiss culture. Both German and English versions I have seen, however, specify that it will perhaps be an English colony, part of the then-growing British Empire. All this is missing from the first versions, for example the first English translation of 1814. The Robinson family in even the first versions, however, have already sprinkled the settlement with European placenames, given in straightforward vernacular in the English translations: "Walrus Island," "Cape Farewell," "Cape Pug Nose," "Flamingo Marsh," "Monkey Grove," "Safety Bay," and so on. The houses and settlements the family build are given names too: "Falconhurst," "Woodlands," "Tentholm," and "Rockburg." These are translated more or less accurately from the German original.

The land of New Switzerland is not taken from "natives." It is rather taken from the animals already there. Nor does the motif of slavery enter in, as it most certainly does in *Robinson Crusoe*. Nor is any hint given of homosociality, such as queer theorists might find in the relation of Crusoe to Friday. Nor is anything present like the slight edge of prurience involved when a young girl enters "the awkward age," such as hovers over the Alice books, as over Henry James's *The Awkward Age*. Until that penultimate episode when Fritz rescues a castaway English girl (she is destined to be a future wife for him), sexuality is wholly absent from *The Swiss Family Robinson*, except as it is implicit in the multiplying of farm animals. Even of the animals, however, nothing whatever is said about their reproduction. The reader is not told, for example, how the sow they save from the wreck comes to produce a swarm of piglets.

The Swiss Family Robinson, in short, when read slowly, *lento*, with a critical eye, reveals itself to be the expression of a definite ideology. This is the ideology of the author, the writer that I as a child wanted to deny even existed, along with the super-added ideologies of all those who augmented the text. This ideology is most strongly reinforced, of course, by the stories themselves, but occasionally it is affirmed overtly, especially in later augmented versions:

> And my great wish is that young people who read this record of our lives and adventures should learn from it how admirably suited is the peaceful, industrious, and pious life of a cheerful, united family to the formation of strong, pure, and manly [!] character.
>
> None takes a better place in the great national family, none is happier or more beloved than he [!] who goes forth from

such a home to fulfill new duties, and to gather fresh
interests around him.

This is from the opening of Chapter 38, "After Ten Years,"
in the Yearling Book edition of *The Swiss Family Robinson*, published by Bantam Doubleday Dell Books for Young Readers
(1999). I have generally cited this edition. The Puffin Classics
edition, source text for the version available on the World Wide
Web (http://www.ccel.org/w/wyss/swiss/swiss.html), has
"those" for "he" and "them" for "him." I wonder who
removed (or substituted) the sexist "he," and when. The later
English versions end with a valedictory address somewhat
similar to the interpolated passage just cited. The later passage
is spoken to Fritz, who is carrying the father's journal to
civilization:

> . . . it is very possible it [the journal] may be useful to other
> young people, more especially to boys.
>
> Children are, on the whole, very much alike everywhere,
> and you four lads fairly represent multitudes, who are
> growing up in all directions. It will make me happy to think
> that my simple narrative may lead some of these to observe
> how blessed are the results of patient continuance in
> well-doing, what benefits arise from the thoughtful
> application of knowledge and science, and how good and
> pleasant a thing it is when brethren dwell together in unity,
> under the eye of parental love.

The last page in the twentieth-century German version I
have obtained has a quite different concluding address to the
reader. It is completely absent from the English versions I have
seen. This passage has, to my ear, a somewhat sinister Teutonic
ring. Though the sentiments are innocent enough, the way

they are expressed makes them sound disquietingly like twentieth-century German propaganda slogans. The passage is a direct apostrophe to Wyss's young readers. I give it first in German, to pay homage to the original language of *Die Schweizerische Robinson*, and for the untranslatable ring of that "Wissen ist Macht, Wissen ist Freiheit, Können ist Glück":

> Euch Kindern aber, die ihr mein Buch lesen werdet, möchte ich noch ein paar herzliche Worte sagen:
>
> "Lernt! Lernt, ihr junges Volk! Wissen ist Macht, Wissen ist Freiheit, Können ist Glück. Macht die Augen auf und seht euch um in der schönen Welt. Ihr glaubt gar nicht, was alles durch so ein paar offne, helle Augen in so einen jungen Kopf hineingeht."

> (But you children, who would read my book, may I still say a couple of heartfelt words:
>
> "Learn! Learn, you young people! Knowledge is power, knowledge is freedom, understanding is happiness. Open your eyes and look around in the beautiful world. You can scarcely believe all the things that enter a young head through a pair of open, clear eyes.")

The Godwin version, closer to the German original of 1812, has a quite different ending, one that has a different ideological exhortation, The final paragraph rejoices in the family's success in creating a model community in the wilderness. Father Robinson thanks Providence "who had so miraculously rescued and preserved us, and conducted us to the true destination of man – to provide for the wants of his offspring by the labour of his hands." The whole text is presented as a journal kept by the castaway Swiss pastor. It ends with the following notation:

> Nearly two years have elapsed without our perceiving
> the smallest traces of civilised or savage man; without
> the appearance of a single vessel or canoe upon the
> vast sea, by which we are surrounded. Ought we then to
> indulge a hope that we shall once again behold the face of a
> fellow-creature? – We encourage serenity and thankfulness
> in each other, and wait with resignation the event!

This is followed by a fictitious "Postscript by the Editor" which tells how an English ship was driven to the island by a storm, made anchor in "Safety Bay," and sent men ashore who were met by Father Robinson alone. He gave his journal to the Lieutenant to give to the Captain. Though plans are made to meet with the whole family the next day, perhaps to rescue them, another violent storm comes up. The English ship has to raise anchor and is driven so far away it cannot return. Only the journal is taken back to civilization.

In this early version, the reader is to imagine the Swiss Family Robinson left indefinitely on their island, like a virtual reality that can be visited only indirectly, in this case through that journal. Endings are decisive for narratives. This original ending gives the whole book a quite different meaning from the modern endings, including the ending in the modern German one I have obtained. These endings all differ from one another, as well as from the endings of *Robinson Crusoe* and *Foe*. The original Godwin ending fits better my childhood conviction that this enchanted island still exists somewhere, though it can be visited only through reading the book. In that somewhere the Robinsons remain forever, always having new adventures and always encountering new animals, plants, birds, and fish.

THE ALICE BOOKS AS DECONSTRUCTION OF
THE SWISS FAMILY ROBINSON

If I had been able to put two and two together at the age of ten, I would have been able to see that Carroll's Alice books, which, as I have said, I had read some years earlier, are the systematic putting in question, or I might even dare to say the "deconstruction," of the certainties so blithely affirmed in *The Swiss Family Robinson*. This is of course no less true, though in different ways, of Coetzee's *Foe*, though the latter was not to be published until fifty years after I first read *The Swiss Family Robinson*. The Alice books center on the situation of a girl, not on a bunch of macho young brothers. Neither Alice's identity, nor the meaning of the strange experiences she has, is ever fixed once and for all. Questions are constantly asked in the Alice books that are never answered. Even the question "Who are *you*?" addressed to Alice by the caterpillar, receives no definitive answer. Alice tells the pigeon she is "a little girl," not a serpent, but she is no longer so sure even of that. In one early moment of distress she fears she has been turned into Mabel, a stupid neighbor girl in the non-Wonderland world. The animals in Wonderland are all fabulous or weird, such as a rabbit with a waistcoat and a watch, or a jabberwock, or a talking egg, or a disappearing Cheshire cat that becomes all grin: " 'Well! I've often seen a cat without a grin,' thought Alice, ' but a grin without a cat! It's the most curious thing I ever saw in all my life!' " These creatures do not fit the predetermined matrices of natural history books, as do the animals in *The Swiss Family Robinson*. A mysterious beast can always be identified, in the latter, as a kangaroo, or an ostrich, or a jackal, or whatever. In *The Swiss Family Robinson* a kangaroo behaves like a kangaroo, but one searches in vain in natural history books for a jabberwock.

None of the maxims and rules Alice has learned from adults are applicable in the Wonderland or looking-glass worlds, whereas the point of *The Swiss Family Robinson* is to show that they do most infallibly work. One synecdochic example of this is what happens, in *Alice's Adventures in Wonderland*, to Isaac Watts's pious eighteenth-century poem praising diligent, God-fearing hard work, modeled on the industry of wild things: "Against Idleness and Mischief" (1715). The original poem sums up perfectly the ethos of *The Swiss Family Robinson*:

> How doth the little busy bee
> Improve each shining hour,
> And gather honey all the day
> From every opening flower! . . .
> In works of labour or of skill,
> I would be busy too;
> For Satan finds some mischief still
> For idle hands to do . . .

In *Alice's Adventures in Wonderland*, however, this becomes, hilariously and subversively, a description of a post-Darwinian "nature red in tooth and claw," not a good model for human behavior:

> How doth the little crocodile
> Improve his shining tail,
> And pour the waters of the Nile
> On every golden scale!
> How cheerfully he seems to grin,
> How neatly spreads his claws,
> And welcomes little fishes in,
> With gently smiling jaws!

The Robinson family is as much like the ravenous crocodile as like the little busy bee, the reader comparing the two poems may reflect. If the Robinsons had encountered a crocodile they would instantly have shot it, as they do a monstrous shark, the lion, the tiger, and so many other creatures. The second son Jack does encounter what he at first thinks is a crocodile, but it turns out to be an iguana. The father entices it into passivity by whistling "a sweet, yet very lively air" to it and tickling it, then snares it and kills it by piercing its nostril. The family then eats it.

As a child, I was happily, as many other children may possibly be, more or less immune to the lessons either of these books taught. I suppose, however, that something seeped in and has helped make me what I am. Nor was I conscious of their dissonance. What I remember most enjoying is the circumstantial reality of these books' imaginary worlds, along with the wonderful ironic destabilizing word play in the Alice books. I also remember liking Through the Looking-Glass rather less well than I liked Alice's Adventures in Wonderland, in spite of my joy in the scene with Humpty Dumpty or the one with the White Knight. Through the Looking-Glass, with its doubts about whether we might not be figments of someone's dream and its ominous allegory of growing up, seemed to me then, as it does today, somehow darker and more threatening than Alice's Adventures. Through the Looking-Glass seems, by comparison to the joyful wildness of Alice's Adventures, foreboding and melancholy. The prefatory poem to Through the Looking-Glass says as much, when it admits that "the shadow of a sigh/May tremble through the story." The last line of the final poem is: "Life, what is it but a dream?" We have heard that said many times, back through the centuries, from Freud to Calderón to Plato. Any direct moral maxims the Alice books proffer, however, were lost on me. That may have made them all the more effective as ideological interpellations.

CONCLUDING PRAISE FOR INNOCENT READING or
IT'S A NEAT TRICK IF YOU CAN DO IT

I claim to have shown that *The Swiss Family Robinson* exemplifies everything I have been saying throughout this book "on literature." Which form of reading do I most commend and recommend? Do I most admire the reading that willingly yields or the one that expects any book will try to perform a brainwash? If the latter, then the book must be interrogated, resisted, demystified, disenchanted, reintegrated into history, especially the history of false ideological confusions. I meant it when I said you must read in both ways at once, impossibly. In the end, however, I confess that I have a forlorn nostalgia, as for something irrevocably lost, for the innocent credulity I had when I read *The Swiss Family Robinson* for the first time. Unless one has performed that innocent first reading, nothing much exists to resist and criticize. The book is deprived beforehand, by a principled resistance to literature's power, of much chance to have a significant effect on its readers. So why read it at all, then, except to satisfy a not wholly admirable joy in destruction, and to keep others from being enraptured, possibly to their detriment? No doubt these resistances to literature have motives quite different from Satan's envy of Adam and Eve's innocent happiness. And yet, are they so different, after all?

Index

anacolythonic.

THINKING IN ACTION – order more now

Available from all good bookshops

Credit card orders can be made on our **Customer Hotlines**:
UK/RoW: + (0) 8700 768 853
US/Canada: (1) 800 634 7064

Or buy online at: www.routledge.com

TITLE	AUTHOR	ISBN	BIND	Prices UK	US	CANADA
On Belief	Slavoj Zizek	0415255325	PB	£8.99	$14.95	$19.95
On Cosmopolitanism and Forgiveness	Jacques Derrida	0415227127	PB	£8.99	$14.95	$19.95
On Film	Stephen Mulhall	0415247969	PB	£8.99	$14.95	$19.95
On Being Authentic	Charles Guignon	0415261236	PB	£8.99	$14.95	$19.95
On Humour	Simon Critchley	0415251214	PB	£8.99	$14.95	$19.95
On Immigration and Refugees	Sir Michael Dummett	0415227089	PB	£8.99	$14.95	$19.95
On Anxiety	Renata Salecl	0415312760	PB	£8.99	$14.95	$19.95
On Literature	Hillis Miller	0415261252	PB	£8.99	$14.95	$19.95
On Religion	John D Caputo	041523333X	PB	£8.99	$14.95	$19.95
On Humanism	Richard Norman	0415305233	PB	£8.99	$14.95	$19.95
On Science	Brian Ridley	0415249805	PB	£8.99	$14.95	$19.95
On Stories	Richard Kearney	0415247985	PB	£8.99	$14.95	$19.95
On Personality	Peter Goldie	0415305144	PB	£8.99	$14.95	$19.95
On the Internet	Hubert Dreyfus	0415228077	PB	£8.99	$14.95	$19.95
On Evil	Adam Morton	0415305195	PB	£8.99	$14.95	$19.95
On the Meaning of Life	John Cottingham	0415248000	PB	£8.99	$14.95	$19.95
On Cloning	John Harris	0415317002	PB	£8.99	$14.95	$19.95

Contact our **Customer Hotlines** for details of postage
and packing charges where applicable.
All prices are subject to change
without notification.

...Big ideas to fit in your pocket